OPPORTUNITIES AND STRATEGIES FOR INDIAN BUSINESS

OPPORTUNITIES AND STRATEGIES FOR INDIAN BUSINESS

Preparing for a Global India

SJ Phansalkar

Response Books
A division of Sage Publications
New Delhi/Thousand Oaks/London

First published in 2005 by

Response Books
A division of Sage Publications India Pvt Ltd
B-42, Panchsheel Enclave,
New Delhi 110 017

Sage Publications Inc
2455 Teller Road
Thousand Oaks
California 91320

Sage Publications Ltd
1 Oliver's Yard
55 City Road
London EC1Y 1SP

Published by Tejeshwar Singh for Response Books, typeset in 10/12 Palatino by Excellent Laser Typesetters, Delhi, and printed at Chaman Enterprises, New Delhi.

Library of Congress Cataloging-in-Publication Data

Phansalkar, SJ (Sanjiv Janardan)
    Opportunities and strategies for Indian business: preparing for a global India/SJ Phansalkar.
        p. cm.
    Includes bibliographical references and index.

1. Management—India. 2. Strategic planning—India. 3. India—Economic conditions—1947– I. Title.

HD70.I4P48 2005   658.4'012'0954—dc22   2004030472

ISBN: 0–7619–3333–6 (HB)   81–7829–490–7 (India HB)
          0–7619–3334–4 (PB)   81–7829–491–5 (India PB)

Production Team: Anupama Purohit, RAM Brown, Mathew PJ, Santosh Rawat

To
my parents,
with affection and gratitude

Sanjiv Phansalkar

CONTENTS

List of tables 9
List of figures 11
List of boxes 13
Preface 15
Acknowledgements 17

Introduction 19

Chapter One 30
*Understanding business response
to economic changes*

Chapter Two 53
The ethos of Indian business houses

Chapter Three 82
*Understanding business strategy
in the Indian context*

Chapter Four 127
Ingredients of the success formulae

Chapter Five 180
*Causes of low performance and failure
in Indian business*

Chapter Six 202
Opportunities and strategies for Indian business

References 220
Index 222
About the Author 232

CONTENTS

List of tables 9
List of figures 11
List of boxes 13
Preface 15
Acknowledgements 17

Introduction 19

Chapter One
Understanding business response
to economic changes 30

Chapter Two
The ethos of Indian business houses 35

Chapter Three
Understanding business strategy
in the Indian context 82

Chapter Four
Ingredients of the success formula 127

Chapter Five
Causes of low performance and failure
in Indian business 180

Chapter Six
Opportunities and strategies for Indian business 202

References 220
Index 222
About the Author 232

LIST OF TABLES

3.1	Competitive tools and their merits	118
4.1	Proactive-reactive continuum and performance	137
4.2	Comparison between high performers and poor performers in six sectors	142
4.3	Comparison on financial parameters	144
4.4	Corporate behaviour regarding change of company name	145
4.5	Introduction of new products	146
4.6	Year(s) when new products were introduced	146
4.7	Relation of the new product to original products	147
4.8	Changes in distribution network	147
4.9	Trade credits	148
4.10	Change in overall production volume	148
4.11	Steps to meet rising production demand and making new products	148
4.12	Other changes in manufacturing to achieve increased capacity	149
4.13	Location and timing of the new factories built	149
4.14	Extent of outsourcing of products/services	149
4.15	Changes in technology	150
4.16	Sources of new technology	150
4.17	Year in which new technology was adopted	150
4.18	Changes in factory layout made	150
4.19	Change of supplier to self-certification for supplies	151
4.20	Adoption of TQM and ISO	151
4.21	Extent of automation	151
4.22	Changes made in organisation	152

4.23   Involvement of external agency in restructuring   152
4.24   New senior management roles created   152
4.25   Composition of the board   152
4.26   Size of employment   153
4.27   Steps for workforce reduction   153
4.28   Cosmo Film Ltd. Finance: PBDIT/Sales and
       PBDT/Sales   158
4.29   Balance sheets as on 31 March   172
4.30   Profit and loss accounts for year ended 31 March   172
4.31   Profit and loss account (Rs in crore)
       non-annualised   173
4.32   Comparison of key parameters showing
       turnaround of CFL   175
5.1   Blunders SSE owners are prone to commit   187
6.1   Typical Indian family business associated
      with successful coping and growth   211
6.2   Patterns of behaviour   216

LIST OF FIGURES

1.1 Triggers, variables and consequences   52
3.1 Products vis-à-vis the market   106
4.1 Organogram   171
5.1 The progression of small enterprises   183
5.2 Highly centralised decision-making   185
6.1 Causes of failure vis-à-vis opportunism   213
6.2 Strategic behaviour vis-à-vis success   213

LIST OF BOXES

2.1 The sordid ethos of Indian business:
    An illustration from the oilseeds industry   68
2.2 Indian business and the way it responded
    to changes in the environment   75
5.1 Glossary of terms used in Table 5.1   189

perhaps, greater need for scholarly attention to understand Indian business than to prescribe to it. I do hope that this book is no more than a small step towards increasing our understanding of Indian business.

PREFACE

The environment experienced by Indian business has been changing over the last 15 years. The stable, if irksome, regime of controls has been replaced by a regime that is evolving and poses many challenges. The last 15 years or so have seen the birth—or, at any rate, the coming of age—of many a potential giant; as well as the decay—or, at times, the death—of some old, venerable businesses. In 2001, I started researching why some Indian businesses coped well with changes brought in by the economic liberalisation. I did find some answers to that query.

This exploration led me, quite imperceptibly, into further exploring why Indian business behaves the way it does. Much as the journalists call it 'India Inc.', I find that Indian business is far from homogenous. I have identified five categories in it: public sector units, MNC subsidiaries, business belonging to 'business families', the businesses set up by technocrats or others not from such families and the myriad, small Indian businesses that run, more or less, like lifestyle enterprises of their owners. The category of businesses belonging to the business families seems to be undergoing the greatest transition.

In this book, I explore and discuss the orientation, tendencies and behaviours of Indian business. I examine whether they behave strategically, and whether behaving strategically lends them a higher probability of sound performance. The classical model of business growing or behaving to a blueprint is, perhaps, unrealistic in a fast-changing environment that poses so many uncertainties as in India. Yet, to me it remains moot whether the preference for opportunism seen in Indian business arises out of this judgement, or whether out of its inherent nature. I think there is, perhaps, greater need for scholarly attention to understand Indian business than to prescribe to it. I do hope that this book is regarded as a small step towards increasing our understanding of Indian businesses.

ACKNOWLEDGEMENTS

A part of this book is based on a research on response of Indian business to liberalization, a research that was generously supported by the ICICI Bank. I express my sincere thanks to them.

Sachin Mardikar, SC Rajsekhar, Chithra Subramaniam and Ananthnarayana Sarma have contributed to the above research and have also, subsequently, sent me feedback on the earlier drafts of this book.

I have profited from the comments and feedback given by a large number of friends and colleagues including Dr KRS Murthy, Tushaar Shah, Vijay Mahajan, MS Sriram, Debiprasad Mishra, Prakash Joshi and an unknown but thorough reviewer. I express my thanks to them.

INTRODUCTION

This book is an attempt to put the developments in Indian business, in a perspective. India is among the fastest growing economies in the world. Rural India has begun getting exposed to products and services of the twenty-first century. The urban and Anglophone business world has only recently woken up to that market. Given these three facets; namely, a growing economy, a hungry rural market and a new realisation about its importance in the business world, the Indian corporate sector is poised to boom. The medium to long-term future of business in India is bright for several reasons that we shall come to, a little later in this book.

There are hiccups, though. The late Nineties saw a spate of events that tested the mettle of Indian business. In fact, since the East-Asian meltdown, one had been hearing pessimistic projections from business leaders—until the economy picked momentum again, in 2003. Pokhran blasts, fall of the government in 1999, the Kargil War, failed monsoons, 9/11 and its global fall out, Gujarat tragedy, the Moody downgrade and the World Bank warning, in 2002, about fiscal mess in the States—all, tended to create an air of pessimism and despair. Economic optimism was at a discount, as India journeyed in the third year of the new century. Finances of the State governments were, and still are, decidedly collapsing. 'Endless dithering interspersed with unexpectedly decisive policy action on the economic front, followed by partial backtracking' at times, thus appeared to be the pattern of policy-making at the Central level during the first, full term of the then coalition rule. The 'serious reservations' about the Common Minimum Programme (CMP) expressed by the Left, barely within a fortnight of its acceptance, suggests that this pattern will probably continue. Constant bickering among the Coalition partners in the national government rules out action on much of the tough economic agenda that pundits suggest. Whether motivated or otherwise, the ratings of Indian currency or other instruments are not flattering. The drought in 2002 had raised the spectre of a famine in Rajasthan. The blithe manner in which people debate whether the Baran deaths were due to malnutrition or starvation, whether people like eating *rotis* made of grass-seeds, and whether eating rats is a part of the traditional food habits in Tamil Nadu and not a result of food shortage, etc. starkly brings home the truth that in some of its elements, the economy has not really moved from the issues it grappled with 30 years ago. Above all, the complete absence of any meaningful public discourse on concerted efforts to pull the country out of the economic morass, rules out any scope for optimism in the medium term. Populism runs full blast. In 2004, three States offered free electricity to the farmers. One State enacted rules requiring private sector firms to have a policy of positive discrimination towards backward classes and has, since then, been busy watering down the provisions when multinational corporations (MNCs) became upset.[1]

While the divestment process moves at an uncertain pace, just no one is talking about the public sector reaching commanding heights any more. Now, much more than ever, the economic fate of the country depends on the vision, dynamism and sagacity of the private sector. How one hopes that these qualities were in abundance! The truth is a little less reassuring. Several businesses show these qualities and some more. We have documented them here, as elsewhere. Yet there is a rather large flip side. The passage of the NPA Bill had made many national dailies begin writing about how the private sector enterprises have been looting the banks.[2] At this juncture it is absolutely important to identify, build, project and support all those who can do well. Do well for themselves, yes; but for the economy as well. And that means we need to understand who can perform well—despite an economic slowdown, despite policy vacuum and despite political instability. This book is an attempt in that direction.

---

[1] See pp. 1–8, *The Economic Times*, 8 June 2004.

[2] Read the series 'The Great Bank Robbery' in *The New Indian Express,* late November 2002.

Opportunities and Strategies for Indian Business also explores and offers explanations about why these solid performers, perform. Journalistic writings on business successes often tend to emphasise the personal qualities of dynamism, courage, leadership and hard work as being the reasons for success. I feel that the soothing imputation of clairvoyance and leadership is seldom an adequate explanation of good performance. Decisions and actions of business companies, rather than a narration of qualities and attributes of business leaders, perhaps, constitute more useful lessons. Some of our views on this subject are based on a study directed towards this. We studied selected companies to see how they managed to do well, even while others faltered. In a sense, this book is in continuation of my earlier work on studying problems and behavioural patterns of Indian firms in the Indian business ethos; and explores reasons why a substantial number of firms seem to be caught in a rut, while others show an ability to meet both—the challenges coming from severe economic conditions and the discontinuities caused by radical policy changes. It throws some light on how companies have survived waves of industrial depressions. Unfortunately it is, perhaps, about learning lessons from the abject fall of the mighty—about how industrial giants of yesteryears have been brought to their knees by the sheer logic of competitive markets. I examine whether the behaviour of Indian business, during the process of economic transition under way for the last 13 years, reveals an underlying pattern of conscious, strategic thinking.

In 2002 I completed a research, generously supported by the then ICICI Limited. This research resulted in the report titled, *'Weathering the Storm: Orientation, Behaviour and Performance of Indian Companies During the Decade of Nineties'*; parts of which are available on the research portal of ICICI Bank Ltd. This research was carried out during 2000–02. Sachin Mardikar assisted me in this research. Prior to that I had studied[3] the way entrepreneurs, who begin in the small industry mode, transit to becoming leaders of formidable industrial groups. This book uses both these researches in addition to the basic body of observations and analysis on which my book on small industry[4] is based. It does so, not the

---

[3] Phansalkar, SJ; *Making Growth Happen*, Response Books, New Delhi, 1999.

[4] Phansalkar, SJ; *How Not to Ruin Your Small Industry*, Response Books, New Delhi, 1996.

least because it depicts the patterns of decision-making that do not seem to be unique only to small industry. Finally, I have used materials obtained from a scan of recent business literature—both, serious and journalistic—pertaining to Indian business.

This book also attempts to examine the relevance of the concepts of business strategy to the way Indian businesses behaved and continue to behave. This becomes relevant for two reasons. In the first place, coping with change—whether successfully or otherwise—is inherently necessary for enterprises in India. The important question is whether this coping behaviour is an instinctive, almost knee-jerk reaction or whether it is rooted in strategies that are well thought-out and deliberated upon. Second, a growing enterprise can of course grow only with the market. Yet, cases of those firms that do exceptionally well and continue to do well for a long time, perhaps, indicate that a well-orchestrated plan or strategy was the basis of their growth. I would like to examine whether the companies whose behaviour indicates the thinking and presence of strategies of this kind, show a performance that is any better than the others. If it does turn out to be so, then there are important lessons for other enterprises.

India during the Nineties

The decade of the Nineties began with difficulties. The Gulf War made things difficult for India. High oil prices, reduced fuel availability, rise in prices of edible oil and a general setback in terms of unsettled conditions made the start of the Nineties quite a bad patch for the country. Perhaps, it is the misfortune of this country that economic hard times and political fluidity had come together. The beginning of the decade saw a weak government that was supported from the outside by the Congress. The government had to face, perhaps, the worst crisis on the Balance of Payment front. It had the unenviable task of negotiating a deal with the Indian Monetary Fund (IMF) to bail the country out of a near-certain default. Then came the minority Congress government that ushered in the first wave of reforms. Dr Manmohan Singh's historic budget ushered in a huge euphoria—arguably, mostly among the economists and the industrial houses. In specific terms, the reforms did away with licensing in all but 18 lines of activity. Regulated foreign exchange regime gave way to an increasingly floating rupee. Current account convertibility boosted confidence of foreign investors and attracted them to India. Barring some sacred cows, like automobiles and sugar; negative lists of imports were more or less abandoned. There was huge reduction in import duties. General policies that set interest rates moving downward were set in motion. Some noise about labour legislation was made. A touch of political realism held this enthusiasm in check.

This euphoria lasted for a full year, before the Ayodhya issue brought about a period of social turmoil and uncertainty. Then came the Harshad Mehta led, stock-price bubble and its subsequent crash, from which the market did not fully recover till the end of the decade. The period, 1992–94, saw a spate of initial public offerings. Entrepreneurs were full of ideas and optimism about the shape of the economy and the opportunities it offered. Quite a few of them were also brimming with the keen desire to make gullible Indian investors part with their money. Yet, a great many projects began in that period. A few examples, perhaps, illustrate the optimism of that period. Encouraged by the de-licensing of the dairy industry, and spurred on by the report of an international consultant, over 80 new units to make dairy products were set up across the country during that time. A research done recently shows that, while many of the entrepreneurs have vanished, many others have folded up. A huge investment was made in creating capacity in the flexible packaging line as well. As is known, the slowdown in Indian economy began sometime in late 1996. An interesting explanation offered states that, as 'Greenfield projects' planned in early Nineties started turning sour, many projects were left starving for investments. Not only did demand coming from this sector collapse, but the money—often obtained by accepting debts—invested in half-complete projects also could not be freed; hence, liquidity was choked. This had a, sort of, cascading effect that was amplified by the East-Asian crisis of 1997. The East-Asian meltdown had disastrous impact on Indian exports. Demand from the East-Asian countries suffered a transient setback and, more importantly, severe erosion in East-Asian currencies made Indian exports relatively unattractive. Then came the Pokhran blasts in 1998 and the 'sanctions' imposed on India thereafter. These sanctions had strong, symbolic meaning. The history is that the rupee did fall from the then level of around Rs 43 to a dollar, to about Rs 44.5 three months after the blast. Finally, the Nineties ended with the Kargil War.

Some important aspects of the economic policy in the new century were: sustained reduction in interest rates, acceptance of the intellectual property rights (IPR) related provisions of the World Trade Organisation (WTO) and, hence, announcement of shift to product patent regime from 2006, simplification and further reduction in direct and indirect taxes, expanding market access to foreign firms in ever-widening areas, easing of norms for foreign direct investment (FDI) in an increasing number of sectors and several moves to do away with Administered Price Mechanism (APM) regime in petroleum products. Yet, reforms have still not reached the States in any significant measures. Where they did, popular anger has struck back as is evident in the polls of 2004. To this day, not one State government has shown the sustained courage to seriously impact the burgeoning and ill-directed subsidies, change the unsustainable cost of governance in the States and make serious attempt to change the protective labour laws.

As far as the Indian private sector is concerned, the following aspects of the reforms are the most relevant:

- It intensified the level of competition in most lines of business. Elimination of the Industrial Licensing regime allowed free entry for Indian players. By progressively reducing tariffs, and by first reducing the sweep-of and, then, finally (in 2001) eliminating the non-tariff (QR type) barriers to trade, the competition to Indian industry from foreign players increased significantly. The cosy and, for the industry, gratifying regime where Indian industry sold what it made to hapless consumers, has gone with the wind; hopefully never to return. Suddenly, Indian industry is required to persuade people to buy what it makes.
- The second aspect of the reform is that the government's profile in major investments has gradually reduced. Not only is the government not setting up new refineries, steel mills, ore processing units, etc., it is also giving up the leadership in infrastructure projects with varying degrees of effectiveness. If the government effort for allowing major interest to

private sector in electricity generation has bombed, the same effort has been very successful in the telecom line. The former has bombed because of the reluctance of most States to untangle the messy knots when it comes to power distribution. The recent road-construction projects (many express ways, the Golden Quadrangle, widening and constructing four lanes on major highways, etc.) on BOOT or BOT basis have really worked miracles in terms of the sheer size of the task taken on, and completed. The implication for the industry, to lobby and 'liaison' with the government, is no longer an effective marketing strategy by itself.

- The third aspect is that a series of capital market reforms measures have made it impossible for promoters of industrial units to go on ignoring the shareholders and ripping their companies. Twenty years ago, some North-Indian industrialists could prevent Lord Swaraj Paul from gaining control on 'their' company. If Lord Paul were fool enough to interest himself in the same companies today, he could do so without any legal hassles. The takeover code now makes it possible for anyone to take over the management of any company.

- The fourth aspect of reforms has been in eliminating a series of irritating and pointless restrictions on what a company can or cannot do. While, earlier, Siemens could not market Bharat Bijlee motors because the proportion of 'traded' goods in their turnover had to be less than so much; today one can run an entire company by 'outsourcing' manufacturing itself.

- Finally, the reform process has certainly brought down the cost of capital to the companies quite significantly.

The Industry's Response to Reforms, as Gleaned by a Layman from Newspaper Reports

Though 'India Inc.' has become a fashionable coinage of the financial press, it is a myth. Indian industry is not homogeneous and does not speak in one language. If one were to stretch the contrast between India and *Bharat* to the commercial world, perhaps there is a sullen *Bharat Maryadit* scowling at India Inc. *Bharat*

Maryadit looks, lives, behaves and misbehaves quite differently from India Inc.—the differences are too stark to be explained away by normal recourse to things like 'minor shades of differences caused by specific interests'. Nevertheless, if one were to schematically caricature the response of the industry to reforms as one could glean from newspaper headlines, one may sum it up as follows:

- Initially, there was a rapturous welcome to the whole concept of liberalisation. Just no one, it seemed, liked the prevailing *neta-babu raj* to borrow another fashionable term to describe the dominance of the government in the economy, till the Nineties.
- Then there was this huge euphoria set into motion by an arguably exaggerated sense of opportunities (the mysterious 250 million strong middle-class that seems to have shrunk in size and has now stopped meriting attention altogether, is just one facet of this) built up and maintained by high-profile consulting firms.
- Simultaneously, there was the haunting fear of impending irrelevance on the part of that section of industry that survived by manipulating the *neta-babu raj*, to suit its own ends. For example, a leading business journal stated, 'While on the one hand, business houses have had to split their assets, often destructively, to take care of the emerging new family environment; on the other hand, they have had to deal with new economic realities—increasing both, domestic competition in the 1980s and international competition in the 1990s. So it is not surprising that at least one-third of the names in the sales list of the top 100 in 1978, did not feature in *Business India*'s list of Super 100 in 1997. Many companies have just disappeared without a trace.'[5] There was also this strong initial resistance to liberalisation that got articulated under what was then called the Bombay Club. The mystical term, 'level playing field' gained currency around that time.
- All throughout, there was a recurrent and, at times, strident demand against liberalisation from specific interest groups.

---

[5] Radhakrishnan, N, and Dutta, S; 'Despair and Hope', *Business India*, 9 March 1998.

Borrowing from Galbraith's[6] writing in his inimitable style, people seemed to feel that, while competition, reforms and liberalisation were wonderful things for the economy as a whole; their specific industry or interest group needed special consideration and continued protection. The sugar industry cited national interests and, with its powerful political clout, managed to avoid reforms for a long time. Cooperative dairy industry screamed blue murder when commercial import of dairy products was allowed; citing the wonderful poverty impacts it was having on Indian farmers. The capital goods' industry let out its near-death rattle, and cited loss of employment as the reason. The drug industry resisted liberalisation as well as the WTO regime—which cited the importance of life-saving drugs in a poor country. Labour unions continue to keep seeing the ghost of the East India Company, everywhere. The small industry has kept lamenting its infamous 'sinophobia'. The message was clear: 'liberalisation is good for everyone else, but I need special protection! Mind you, I need it not because I want to remain cosy and comfortable, but to protect national interests of some supremely important kind.'

- Then, of course, there were those who made serious attempts to grapple with the challenges thrown up by the liberalisation process. It is this group that we wish to study and talk about, further on. We need to realise that the challenges posed to Indian companies did not come from the liberalisation process alone. The flattening out of demand in mid-Nineties, the East-Asian meltdown, and the post-Pokhran sanctions—all, together, have caused a long period of slowdown that began around 1997, and did not quite end till the upswing of 2003. Thus, what Indian firms saw in the Nineties was a combination of liberalisation and a prolonged slowdown.

The actual behaviour of individual firms presented, and continues to present, a mixed and a confusing picture. Some simply sold out. We had companies owning well-established brands (like Gold Spot or Kelvinator), selling out to foreign competitors. Some sulked for a long time but, then, took decisive actions to build on

---

[6] Galbraith, JK; *Almost Everyone's Guide to Economics*, Penguin, London, 1978.

their strength. Some others exhibited peculiar choices: a national business-house went in for the marketing of household furniture. Some small industrialists looked the world in its eye and made it wilt. Some others, still, surprised everyone by shaking off the rust and lethargy, to take up highly competitive positions.

The Questions

I wish to raise certain questions in this context.

In the first place, *did Indian companies behave 'strategically', at all, during this time? Or were they essentially opportunistic? Who behaved strategically and who behaved opportunistically? Can one associate better performance with strategic behaviour (or putting it another way, does the strategic-opportunistic continuum have any relationship with a sustained, good performance; even during bad times?)* Going a step further: does strategic behaviour have any place, at all, in the Indian business environment or does somewhat deliberate opportunism double up as strategy? These questions are not about mere semantic quibbling. The term, 'strategic behaviour' has a specific meaning in business literature. It connotes a blueprint, a long-term plan about how the firm expects to see its business unfold. It indicates that the developments in and about the firm are a product of conscious and deliberate choice made by the firm keeping such a long-term plan at the forefront. Opportunistic behaviour, on the other hand, indicates that an individual or a firm lives, more or less, by the moment or, at least, cares not to think long-term, is concerned much more with 'here and now' type questions, seeks to grab opportunities when they come and may, perhaps, not mind being a shade lax as far as regulations and rules are concerned. While the imports of these terms are broadly understood, there could be a range of behaviour within each category. Strategic behaviour does not exclude tactical adjustments, but does so without diverting from the chosen course. We shall discuss this in detail, again.

The second question is, *how do Indian businesses look at changes in their environment? Do they behave like vested interests that feel threatened with such changes and, hence, react to forestall, obviate, deflect, dilute or blunt these changes?* Or do they look at these changes as opportunities for ushering in transformations within themselves for increasing their competitiveness? Again, what factors determine who responds reactively and who takes the changes as opportunities?

I devote some space to discussing the factors that have led to successful performance, as well as factors that have led to stagnation and failure of businesses in the Indian context. I do try to relate these factors to the strategic vis-à-vis opportunistic postures of businesses. Hence an important question that I explore is, *what determines how a specific business behaves when faced with rapidly changing economic environment?*

Chapter One

UNDERSTANDING BUSINESS RESPONSE TO ECONOMIC CHANGES

Understanding How Business Responds to Changes in the Environment

An implicit assumption in the whole discussion about growth propensity, about strategy of a company and the competitive strategy, is the relative stability of the environment. That is, *ab initio*, formulation of the strategy or the competitive strategy takes place as if the extant environment will remain frozen. Clearly, it does not. The environment keeps changing in myriad different ways. While completely incidental or trivial changes may not require any response from the business, some changes do. It is important to understand how the business responds to such changes, how it adjusts its competitive strategy or its basic strategy in the light of the changes in the environment, to what extent it changes its actions, in which spheres of its activity it does so, in which spheres of its behaviour it avoids or resists changes, what thought processes cause such changes, and so on. I discuss, below, diverse theoretical ways to address this question. Different scholars have adopted a number of different approaches to explain the behaviour of businesses. I discuss and sum up a selection from rich and instructive scholarly work on this subject. In doing so, I have restricted myself to those works which have directly addressed the question of how businesses respond to changes in their environment.

In microeconomics, it is believed that a firm maximizes profits in the short-term and investor wealth in the long-term.[1] In elementary expositions, one assumes perfect information, omniscient and capable analytical ability and certainty. In more realistic formulations, one argues that the firm amasses all possible information and makes rational decisions on resource allocation, using elaborate calculus that incorporates treatment of risk and uncertainty. Multiplicity of goals is ignored or handled neatly, by arguing for evolution of a single optimand that combines different utilities inherent in the multiple goals; or, at times less neatly, by attempting to define acceptable trade-offs between crucial goals.

When one 'opens up' the organisation, the assumption that business firms behave in a manner that is directed by their goals turns out to be really naïve. I have already listed some of the related issues. There are many strands of thinking even in the organisation theory framework, about how businesses respond to changes in their economic environment. I select a few of these for discussion as they relate more closely to my main argument. The 'behaviour' of a business is the confusing totality of all its small and big actions in diverse arenas (such as finance, production, governance and marketing). In general, it is good to believe that most overt business behaviour is oriented towards meeting the firm's goals and objectives. This, too, could be a bit naïve. Each arena of action is manned, for the firm, by a group of individuals. The business behaviour results from the actions of these individuals. It would, indeed, be a coincidence if each of these individuals were also fired by the zeal to meet the firm's objectives. Even if it were so, there still would be a question about the congruence in the way each interpreted the objectives.

Even if we ignore these real, behavioural issues in implementation, the link between business goals/objectives and actual behaviour is not direct, nor clear. There may be multiple goals. Their priority (*entre-se*) in a conflict situation may not have been

---

[1] See e.g., Samuelson, Paul A, and Nordhaus, William; *MicroEconomics*, McGraw Hill, 2001.

explicitly resolved. Often, these goals are not explicitly stated. Even when they are, there are numerous cases of a hiatus between the stated and the operative goals. Hence an observer has no choice but to 'derive' the operative goals, by the route known to economists as the revealed preference. In effect, this is what I attempt later. I attempt to see the overt behaviour, understand it and derive operative intents there-of and, then, make inferences about the orientation of the firms.

To begin with, I try to present different ways adopted by various scholars for looking at how businesses respond to the economic changes that they experience. Some of them are straight from scholarly books, while some others blend my observations and conjectures with theory. Yet, all of them really explain or predict behaviour from the point of view of an external observer.

Classical contingency theorists look at three aspects of the environment and attempt to predicate the organisation's response to them. They are aspects of heterogeneity, stability and competition for resources. The task environment of an organisation poses contingencies and uncertainties, both of which detract from efficiency. Hence, under norms of rationality, as Thompson[2] puts it, organisations tend to devise ways of adapting so as to protect their core from the disturbing influence of the environment.

An organisation facing heterogeneous environment, it tries to categorize the environment, into relatively homogeneous segments. It assigns work pertaining to these segments to boundary-spanning units, designed to exchange with each homogeneous segment. When the environment is stable, its demands are completely predictable and the attention shifts to achieving efficiency in meeting the demands. But when the environment is turbulent, it is necessary to constantly watch for the changes and take quick action to protect the core. Hence, unlike the case when the environment is stable, power within the organisation shifts to the boundary-spanning unit and the attention is on achieving a high speed of response to changed demand—rather than a highly efficient response to predictable demand. Such organisations tend to invest in predicting changes in the environment, in trying to influence it and in keeping a portfolio of contingency plans; ready to be put into action at a short notice. Logically therefore, the organisation

---

[2] Thompson, JD; *Organizations in Action*, Prentice-Hall, Englewood Cliffs, 1967.

would postpone hard, irreversible investments as much as possible but generate reserves that can be invested. One may use these basic postulates to project what an organisation will do when the nature of its environment begins to change. An organisation faced with an undifferentiated and homogeneous environment at all times would, at first, grope a bit when faced with emerging heterogeneity; but would eventually take the most natural course as the one predicted. When the stable environment facing an organisation suddenly turns turbulent, it would bound to be substantially disoriented for a while, before it devises mechanisms (like those previously discussed) to deal with this turbulent environment.

The other aspect of an organisation's environment is the relative demand and supply for resources and/or markets. Thompson uses the term 'support capacity', for both these. Logically, when the support capacity is widely dispersed but demand for it is concentrated, monopolistic behaviour emerges. When the support capacity is concentrated but demand is dispersed, then monopsonist conditions emerge; and when both the availability and demand for support are widely dispersed, more or less free market conditions prevail. Different predictions are made about the organisation's behaviour under these conditions. When the support capacity is concentrated and the organisation is crucially dependent on entities offering such support, it then seeks to build alliances with them or to make other arrangements to ensure stable support. Such cooperative strategies include contracting, coalescing or co-opting. A purely competitive strategy of maintaining a large number of alternatives is used when both, the support capacity as well as demand, are dispersed.

Contingency theorists have also discussed how goals are determined in an organisation, and who determines them. Thompson discusses realistic constructs of dominant coalition and inner circle in organisations. These are essentially loose groups of individuals having the formal authority, informal power or need-based discretion and can, hence, influence the organisational action. Goals are viewed essentially as resultants of a process of negotiation among the members of these groups. In that sense, goals lose all their pristine permanence and become fluid and dynamic. If goals themselves become fluid and dependent upon situations, conventional argument, that firms behave in the manner determined by their goals, loses all its significance.

Simon's close associates Cyert and March[3] had mooted, in their famous behavioural theory, the question of how organisations decide and respond. They had suggested that organisations are adept at behaving in well-marked patterns. These patterns—call them routines or standard operating procedures—are essentially designed to enable the organisation's staff to meet the demands of their everyday chores—smoothly and efficiently. When the organisation finds that its routines no longer work the way they are expected to, it does not engage in a wide and sweeping investigation of causes, consequences and the best ways of responding; but instead, engages itself in a search that allows it to meet the new problem (the trigger) in the quickest and the cheapest manner. If the change that had rendered original routines ineffectual is lasting, then routines are modified on a sustained basis. Else, the original routines take over at the very moment when the trigger that caused the anomaly vanishes. Such a problemistic search is merely aimed at solving the problem so the organisation can return to its set and patterned ways, and is not aimed at optimising on any goals. In this sense, they negate the postulate of conventional theory that firms seek to maximize or optimise profits or wealth or any such thing.

Alisson[4] offers a wonderful exposition of diverse theories of decision-making that have direct relevance to organisational response. The belief that organisations respond depending upon their quick assessment of how an event in the environment affects the objectives of the organisation, is essentially rooted in the rational-economic model of organisation. There are many 'ifs and buts'. Drawing from the discussion in Alisson's work, 'fidelity' of the action of the individuals who act, is a function of:

- How well these goals have been communicated to them,
- How well they have understood them,
- How their micro-dimensions have been impacted by the specific sub-environment impacting upon the arena,
- What the degree of congruence between the individuals' preference and these goals is, and

[3] Cyert, R and March, JG; *Behavioural Theory of the Firm*, Prentice-Hall, Englewood Cliffs, NJ, 1963.

[4] Alisson Graham T; *Essensce of Decision*, Harvard University Press, 1971.

- What the extent of formal discretion is, and what is the informal power they enjoy within their firms.

Alisson adds an additional 'political dimension' to the discussion of how the individuals will act. Inevitably, there will be cliques within an organisation—each one jockeying to have its interests protected, furthered, etc. Individuals in an organisation are prone to view and interpret the trigger they see from the environment, in the light of how it affects the interests of the clique to which they belong and how the interests of that clique can be protected or furthered in the process of responding.

Steinbruner[5] goes one step further and suggests a *cybernetic model of the firm*. Rooted in the work of Weiner[6] this strand compares organisations with the functioning of the animal brain. To start with, let us understand the behaviour of Norbert Weiner's cat. This cat is sitting cosily on a carpet, in front of a fire. Now, supposing that the fire is becoming less intense, the cat makes small adjustment to its posture to make itself more comfortable despite the decreased heat. It does not give up its position within the room, only makes small adjustments. This is the 'micro-control' loop governed behaviour, and is appropriate till such a time as when small, tactical changes in the cat's posture are adequate to meet the challenges thrown by the changes occurring around it. When even this does not provide relief to the cat, it, simply, gets up and goes to sit closer to the fire. Notice, here, that the original position—vis-à-vis the fire—was given up; and a new position was searched, appropriated and used. This is the macro-control loop governed behaviour that makes for more substantial and long-lasting changes. From this is derived the elaborate and conceptually rich cybernetic theory of decision-making. It says very little about the essential goals for which the organisation arranges itself; but once these goals are formed, the theory argues that subsequent behaviour is essentially based on feedback control. There is a micro-control loop that seeks to induce small tactical changes in what and how the firm does. When these do not seem adequate, the firm transits to the macro-control loop in which

[5] Steinbruner; *Cybernetic Theory of The Firm*, Princeton University Press, Princeton, NJ, 2002.
[6] Weiner, Norbert; *Collected Works*, MIT Press, 2001.

aspects that cut across several functions and have longer term lives and whose effects are evaluated and implemented. It may be instructive to visualize a nested sequence of such loops. The most basic loop of feedback control deals with performance of everyday tasks of an identified group of people, in a specific functional area. The most comprehensive 'mega' feedback control loop pertains to the performance of the entire organisation—in relation to its complex and multiple goals—over a period of time. It is easy to see that the cybernetic model depicts a naïve and not a strategic animal. It describes just the response to change and does not take into account forward thinking, predicting, projecting or advance planning. The cat does not assess whether and how fast the fire will die down, nor does it make a contingency plan; it simply adapts to the fire as it mellows down. Thus, each loop activates as and when the need arises, and it becomes easy to see the direct relevance of this way of conceptualising organisations.

Industry Response to Economic Changes and Recession

The discussion so far focused on how different scholars posited about the way organisations respond when faced with changes in their business environment. Economic slowdown, sluggish demand, intensified competition and recession are different types of environmental phenomena that organisations have been facing in this country, during the last 15 years or so. It is, perhaps, interesting to speculate what these various concepts imply and predict for the businesses that are faced with such changes. Contingency theorists suggest an interesting behaviour. Suppose an organisation has faced a stable and predictable demand for its products, this demand often far outstripping the supply (as was typically the case with cement, steel, scooters, caustic soda, aluminium and a host of other commodities witnessing a 'shortage'. This is what a lot of large industrial houses, in India, revelled in for decades.) Organisations, in such cases, tended not to worry about product improvement, but focused on achieving efficiency in logistics and other operations. When even prices were controlled, these efforts led often to a focus on cost reduction disregarding quality. As the environment changed 'suddenly' (faster than what the organisation could adjust to, that is), organisations had to adjust. A series of tie-ups for marketing as well as in consolidation, are evidence of such cooperative behaviour. Competitive behaviour, on the other hand, finds evidence in diversifying the marketing effort—from it being purely domestic, to third country trade as well. Cybernetic theory, too, seems to have ready applications to the situation. An example illustrates this point: a company selling a specific class of products—say, scooters—notices that the market is becoming sluggish. It makes the micro-control loop adjustments of price-cuts, promotional schemes and small product modifications. Discovering that this is ineffective and the market is shifting towards lighter scooters, it introduces the lightweight, self-starting scooters and multiplies the product range within this category. When this, too, fails to stem the rot, it introduces the changes dictated by 'macro-control loop', introduces motorbikes of the kind it never made before and, significantly, enters the export market. Clearly, neither the model nor our illustration helps us define the goal of the scooter company. For this way of modelling organisation behaviour, goals are, sort of, a given. We may derive, via the revealed preference route, that the firm's goal was to continue to maintain its position in the two-wheeler market.

However, we need to find out how have industrial units actually behaved when faced with changes in economic environment they face. I now turn to a few studies that address the actual manner in which organisations have responded.

Geroski and Gregg[7] have studied the way recession affects businesses, and the way business firms respond to recession. The authors say that economic theory would argue that in times of recession (that is, the periods during which the aggregate demand, and hence in-general demands for any given firms; falls), firms would reduce both, output and prices, to achieve new balance. These reductions would be determined by the supply curves pertaining to the products in question. Second, the nature of costs of adjustment (whether they can be graduated costs or there are fixed costs of making any change at all) will tend to influence the nature of response. Huge fixed costs of adjustments will tend to

---

[7] Gersoski, PA, and Gregg, P; *Coping With Recession*, Cambridge University Press, Cambridge, 1997.

encourage firms to try and 'see through' the smaller depressions, etc. These statements represent a shade too general an expectation. Recession may not affect all the firms equally. According to their own assessment, no more than 10 per cent of the firms that the authors surveyed, claimed to have been affected, 'extremely severely', by recession. Thus, there is a difference in the way recession affects different firms. Also, not all firms behave in an identical manner. Some firms may have grown faster and added facilities and staff during the periods of boom that preceded the recession. Such firms may have a greater need to make adjustment. Others, who followed a more conservative approach during the boom, may have much less need to adjust. The authors report that there is much greater tendency to reduce costs, such as staff costs, etc., among firms affected by recession; but this tendency is the commonest among firms affected very severely. Often, some of these firms may sell off lines of activities and, thus, hive off major investments and costs since they wish to achieve focus. Firms tend to cut investments in factories and buildings much more severely, than in advertising or in research and development. The authors find only a partial support for the general belief that firms that survive a recession emerge leaner and fitter from it. The authors find that firms certainly emerge leaner: there is a great deal of job shedding that is done by almost all firms and, certainly, by those firms affected most severely by the recession. Yet, quite a lot of this job shedding is of the nature of 'letting the skills hoarded during boom times, out of the firm'. Whether these firms emerge fitter, in the sense of being more able to meet competitive pressures better, is moot. The authors argue that there are three major ways of encouraging the firms to become fitter: in the first place, there is the normal competition in the product-market. Second, there are the pressures for achieving efficiency caused by capital market pressures of mergers and acquisitions. Finally, come the recession-led developments that result in accentuating the competition in every industry and, thus, causing firms to become more efficient. In the view of the authors, recession may not be the optimal way for firms to become fitter. The way these authors succinctly put it, 'recessions are useful to social scientists interested in finding 'natural experiments' which help them analyse what happens to firms in crisis, but they are probably not good for much else!' (Geroski and Gregg, p. 153).

Literature on actual business response to changes in economic environment in India is not rich. Some work has been done on how firms cope with liberalisation process as well. Khandwala[8] came to the conclusion that, till 1995, the Indian corporate world seemed to have coped reasonably well with liberalisation—judging from the increases recorded in exports and in corporate profits till then. He suggested that this could be attributed in part to the phased and slow manner of introducing the changes in India as opposed to the 'shock therapy' to which some East-European countries were subjected and in part to the strong entrepreneurial tradition in India. He suggested that for a specific firm, response to liberalisation needed to be in part systemic and in part strategic. Systemic response meant introducing changes in organisation's management style, organisation culture, etc. The strategic response would be in terms of choosing/modifying the product-market posture, and taking competitive position by adopting one or a combination of generic competitive strategies. Another work of note is a recent book by Dr Palande.[9] He discusses how Indian industry responded to liberalisation. Industry is central to a country's economic prosperity. Independent India inherited a fledgling industry and widespread social disparity. The new government at that time adopted a mixed economic model, with a view to nation building, and took upon itself the responsibility of planning industrial growth and regulating the economy. In time and with successive governments, the regulations became controls. The huge, public sector enterprises, initially set up to give a boost to the core industries, proliferated and became unprofitable and unwieldy. Together with bad governance, restrictive industrial and trade policies, and poor financial management, the industrial growth was slow and development was distorted. The economic model did not achieve its well-meaning social objectives and, in the early Nineties, the country found itself facing a financial and economic crisis. On the advice of the World Bank and the International Monetary Fund, economic reforms were introduced in a phased manner. These aimed to stabilise the economy in the short-term, and to create conditions for a sustainable growth

---

[8] Khandwala, PN; 'Effective Corporate Response to Liberalization. The Indian Case'. *The Social Engineer*, 1996: 2.

[9] Palande, PS; *Coping with Liberalisation: The Industry's Response to New Competition*, Response Books, New Delhi, 2000.

in the long-term, through better financial management and policy changes. The new economic policy sought to reduce government interference in economic matters and, in essence, intended to make the industry and trade breathe freely. Restrictive policies gave way to liberalisation from both, within and without. Dr Palande, having thus educated the reader in the introductory chapters of his book on liberalisation, makes an attempt to follow what happened thereafter. At the macroeconomic level, the first task was to bridge the gap between demand and supply, and control the spiralling inflation rates. Huge budgetary deficits, internal and external debts had to be lowered, and the dwindling foreign exchange reserves had to be stocked up. The stabilisation measures introduced did meet their short-term objectives. For long-term reforms, the Structural Adjustment Programme, a reforms package model proposed by the World Bank, was adopted. Fundamentally, it aimed to deregulate the Indian economy and merge it with the world economy. Changes were broadly introduced in areas of industrial licensing, the Monopolistic and Restrictive Trade Practices (MRTP) Act, small-scale industries, public sector, taxation, banking, insurance, corporate laws, government expenditure, export-import policies, foreign investments and technology agreements. The book effectively engages each of the topics, across several chapters. The main focus of the book lies in the four chapters devoted to how the industry actually responded to liberalisation. It was feared that liberalisation, with the entry of big players, would most hit the small-scale industries; as they, with their low technology base, inadequate flow of credit and restricted reach to the market, were the least competitive. Dr Palande devotes several sections to these problems. He suggests that the apprehension of small-scale industries, that they would be wiped out in the face of competition, is unfounded as their product lines are usually different from large industries. Moreover, the small-scale industries could thrive in a symbiotic relationship with large industries as ancillaries. Unfortunately not much is presented on the current situation of the old and the new small-scale industries.

The medium and large-scale industries, according to Dr Palande, have reacted to liberalisation in many ways:

a) Those industries that were in business just because they could get a government licence, and thrived on subsidies with no emphasis on the quality of product and services, find themselves in a spot and face closures or takeovers. They are the most vociferous opponents of liberalisation.

b) In contrast, quality manufacturers or service providers who were willing to change their policies according to the marketability of their product or services in the face of competition, were not only able to survive, but also showed a sharp growth.

c) Industrial houses that had diversified into various sectors, are presently trying to consolidate into areas in which they are most competent. Changes in management style, increased inputs in R&D, better quality control and investment in employee welfare are some of the strategies adopted by them. Large industrial houses consider competition from the external sources to be more potent than that from domestic sources. They feel that the process of liberalisation should be slowed down, so that they have more time to adjust to competition. This issue has political overtones, as the entry of MNCs has revived, in some quarters, the *swadeshi* sentiments of the pre-Independence era.

This assessment of how the Indian firms have responded is a 'view from the top' and has tended to be influenced by general observations. Had it been significantly substantiated by concrete instances, of action taken by specific industrial units or industrial houses, it would have offered rich insights in the behaviour of Indian business.

S Roy[10] has noted that economic liberalisation brought in more munificent changes for businesses. While these changes created opportunities for larger growth and better returns, they also intensified the competition. Based on a survey of 110 firms, he notes that Indian industry has responded by:

- Aiming for higher growth and better returns,
- Increasing the scale of operations,
- Diversifying in new products and business lines,
- Expanding geographically, both in domestic and export markets,

---

[10] Roy, S; FPM Thesis, 'Strategic Response of Firms to Economic Liberalization', submitted at IIM Ahmedabad, 2002.

- Widening the product range, and
- Sharing the tangible and intangible resources across business units.

He reports that a firm that has a dominant line of activity, with moderate diversification, seems to respond and do better than either firms that have a single business line or firms that are over-diversified. Younger and smaller firms responded better and fared better compared to old and large firms, possibly due to 'organisational inertia'. He did not find ownership of the firm to be a significant influence on response or performance.

As expected, liberalisation has brought in opportunities that have made many firms take to them with ambition and optimism. Recessions and economic threats force people to tighten their belts and take actions that make them leaner and meaner. This is the summary of what has been mentioned. I feel that most of the work cited prior to this, looks at business firms responding to economic changes without 'opening up' the firms. This is, in some way, natural; since the effort to open up the firm involves process-oriented study on what, how and why people within the firm do what they do. This kind of study takes time and can look at only smaller samples. There is a great deal of value in learning about the processes, the thinking and the exchanges that occur within the organisations which are confronted with change, and which must respond in a meaningful manner. I submit that one may be able to get some evidence on the reality of the organisational response to change but, to an extent, it becomes necessary to project, conjecture and hypothesise.

Strategic Vs Opportunistic Behaviour

If the ways of looking at how businesses respond to changes in their environment are based on scholastic works; the views to follow are based on somewhat earthy, though pragmatic, blends of observations and conjectures. The first one is an attempt to get the adjectives right. It explores the meaning of the adjectives—strategic behaviour and opportunistic behaviour—and assesses how much of a contrast there really is between these two.

I shall interpret the words 'strategic behaviour of business' in the same sense as is understood in conventional courses of business policy. I devote significant space to it later in Chapter three. Here, I suffice it to say that a firm behaves in a manner consistent with a deliberate and well-considered strategy (or simply 'behaves strategically' for simplicity) if its decisions tend to reinforce:

- Its conscious (even if not explicit to outsiders) choice of mission (definition of its business and goals therein, product-market posture and time, and space-bound goals within them, etc.) and
- The pattern of actions in moving towards it.

I am sure that the common parlance meaning of the word 'opportunistic' is understood well. There is something infra-dig about that meaning. In an aside, one may note that, irrespective of their precise dictionary meaning, words come to acquire strong value-connotations by their sheer, repeated usage in a particular context. For instance, the term 'vested interest' is actually a value-neutral term. When, in a particular constellation of circumstances, I see continued benefit to me, I have a vested interest in their continuance. As long as I do not adopt extra-legal or unethical methods to force the continuation of status quo, my vested interest should not considered to be anti-social. But in India, the words 'vested interest' are commonly used as an epithet to describe a group of individuals, adept at using all possible methods to continue the status quo so that they derive benefits from it. Hence, we take the term to mean something inherently bad and anti-social. The same thing is, perhaps, applicable to the words opportunism and opportunistic behaviour. In this connotation, opportunistic behaviour is the grabbing, 'carpet-bagging' behaviour of undignified and cheap people. There is something 'grab-the-chance-when-no-one-is-look-ing' about it. Dignified pillars of economy and business are not 'supposed to be' opportunists. Their behaviour is not expected to be opportunistic.

I do not mean to use the words opportunism and opportunistic with these value connotations. Somehow, these words seem to create the images of what I just narrated. I mean opportunistic behaviour merely as an antonym of strategic behaviour.

I examine, more closely, the range of behaviours that are broadly indicated by the term opportunistic.

At the 'lowest' end is the sheer opportunism of the small and petty businessmen. Auto-rickshaw drivers in Chennai or Bangalore or taxi drivers in Delhi (all over, in fact; but those in these cities are especially notorious) identify a man unfamiliar with the city and overcharge him to the extent they can. This behaviour is at its most visible at ill-connected railway stations, such as the Kurla and Bandra termini in Mumbai. In a similar vein, one may see a petty, toyshop owner jack up the price of a cheap toy on seeing how a child is bent upon having that toy, and also how the child's mother cannot afford to have him bawling in the midst of the market. This really is the 'naïve opportunism' of the businessman who does not expect to have to transact with the very same customer a second time.

The infamous and not yet dead practice of 'black marketing' of products and services is, perhaps, the next level. Earlier on in the shortage ridden Indian economy, everything was as easily available in the black market as it was difficult to get it at the 'official' price. The businessman knows that the customer desperately needs the product, and has no option but to pay extra and is quite unlikely to 'squeal' on him. Hence he can overcharge. Usually the premium, the so-called 'on' money, has always been taken in cash so that there is no evidence of its ever having changed hands.

At the same level, perhaps, is the rent-seeking behaviour of government officials and politicians. Speed moneys and bribes are so common as to have become 'standardised' in most walks of life. Try and sell a flat or a house in any city, and you are quickly told how much it will cost you to get various documents from the relevant authorities. Both these categories—the black marketer and the corrupt government men—are exploiting the urgency and then helplessness of those who want the goods, services or clearances. Legal as well as ethical issues are involved here, and it is best to stop further exploration of this category of opportunism.

These three types of behaviour earn for the word opportunism its unsavoury image.

At the first legitimate level, may be the opportunism of the small food-products sellers who encircle a bus held up at a railway crossing, waiting for a train to pass. They have seen this to be a wonderful spot to sell some food products (seasonal fruit, chips, peanuts, cold drinks, etc.); bought typically, in an instant, by

it could be a subsidiary of a foreign company. In either event it is not a unit of decision-making but just one of the arms of a larger group. Let us look at how the business would respond to the economic changes in India, had it been an MNC arm. While I quite agree that the economic changes here are never irrelevant for a business operating here, their 'larger than life' perception holds true only for those who are confined to this country. Businesses that are either arms of MNC or are associates of MNCs are bound to be objects of decision-making by their respective parents. The MNC compares the economic opportunities and costs it experiences in different countries, and decides its future course in India using this comparative picture. Often the Indian arm is too insignificant a part of the global business, and may be given in the charge of someone who really cannot pull his weight in the parent's headquarters. (To caricature this, I say that the MD of the Indian arm reports to the secretary of the third assistant vice-president in the department of Asia-Pacific Region.) When the economic changes are seen as causing more irritation and pain than opportunities, and when the boss is a lightweight; often, the parent simply decides to get rid of the Indian arm. The Indian arm is sold to someone else, usually to another MNC. Point is, the behaviour of such a company in India is influenced by factors other than the changes in economic environment in India alone. Some of these factors may be known only to the management of the parent, and not to an Indian observer.

When the focal company is a member of a group of companies controlled by the same management, the behaviour of the focal company cannot be seen as self-contained or independent. Obviously, the management is looking after the group's total interests and hence the behaviour of the focal company is a subset of the total business response. A case in point is found in several Information Technology (IT) related companies of the Tata empire. I, myself, almost made the mistake of studying only one of them as if it were stand-alone. That focal company was both, an MNC affiliate as well as a member of a large group of companies. To view the behaviour of the company as comprising a total response to the business environment was obviously an error.

In summary, how a business responds to changes in the business environment is as much a function of the changes that are, in fact, occurring outside as of the lineage of the focal business and the objectives of its parents. And since many other factors hinted at, may be relevant, the response is indeterminate, unpredictable.

Inward Looking and Reactive, or Outward Looking and Proactive?

Changes, of any type, are always disquieting. Sometimes, they may be threatening. A young man, full of confidence and energy, bubbles with enthusiasm when the boss transfers him to a new city. An apple-shaped father of two children may feel very threatened by the same prospect. The same is perhaps true for businesses. Some businesses are 'young'—lean, adaptable and full of the urge to take the world in their stride. Others are more 'weathered and old', have risk-averse and stodgy managers, have rusted ways of working, etc. They feel threatened by changes in their economic environment. Yet, they have vested interests (please note, I use this term non-pejoratively) in the existing business situation. Robert Merton[11] offers a useful model to characterize how a group behaves when its vested interest is threatened with potential changes in its environment. He suggests that such a group behaves in a pattern:

- In the first place, it denies the very need for these changes and paints how these changes would make matters they are supposed to cure; far worse than they be at that time.
- Then the group takes recourse to some super-ordinate objective ('defence of fatherland' or 'protection of traditional values', or in the Indian case, 'national self-interest') to raise such objections that changes the level of debate.
- When these polemics do not help and some concrete action has to be taken up, the group members make such ornamental changes as would take the steam off the arguments of the proponents of the change.
- Finally, when forced to take real action, the group takes such action as would protect the core of its entrenched interests while adapting to the changes.

---

[11] Merton, RK; *Social Theory and Social Structure*, Amerind, New Delhi, 1968.

We find that this pattern may describe some of the behaviour and response of the Indian corporate world. The 'Bombay Club' did make noises often enough. *Swadeshi* protagonists, who may or may not act as fronts for some business interests, routinely let out repeated cry about multinationals controlling everything in India. There has been a major brouhaha about 'cultural aggression'. The holy cow of the Fifth Column has resisted successfully the freeing of investment in print media for a long time using such reasons. A huge xenophobia spread about Chinese imports was also unleashed at the time of freeing Quantitative Restrictions (QR). Whatever be the merits of the arguments in these individual instances, they fall in the category of the behaviour suggested by Merton. Such is the behaviour of a 'reactive group'.

A proactive group may act the way Khandwala[12] suggested. He suggested that for a specific firm, response to liberalisation needed to be in part systemic and in part strategic. Systemic response meant introducing changes in organisation's management style, organisation culture etc. Strategic response would be in terms choosing/modifying product-market posture and taking competitive position adopting one or a combination of generic competitive strategies.

To capture this dimension of behaviour, I propose a simple model:

Depending on how the management of a company looks at the broad things like economic policy, it could act in diverse ways. Some of them may keenly anticipate the policy outcomes, and choose a course of action that helps them the most according to what they anticipate. Some may actually take the trouble of lobbying to see if what they had wanted or anticipated did, actually, happen in the policy arena. Some other managers may not worry too much about these things, but may think of more immediate things as they happen. An organisation theorist remarks that if a CEO of a US-based company does not take notice and swing into action when he finds his best customer playing golf with his fiercest competitor, he, the CEO, does not deserve to be where he sits! While driving a car, you may think about the level-crossing two kilometres away; but you will focus, more clearly, on the guy who is rashly overtaking you! Essentially, the question is

---

[12] Khandwala, PN; op. cit.

when, after what external event, does a manager take notice and act. Such an event is what we call a trigger.

In general, the changes in the business environment would serve as 'triggers' for the organisation. A company usually tries to assess the adequacy of its current behaviour. It tries to figure out whether what it is doing is fine. If not, it wishes to modify some part of its actions. If companies know that Maharashtra is entering a prolonged phase of power shortage, and if their production operations are very crucially dependent on smooth and continuous power supply; chances are that a lot of them will make appropriate back-up arrangements. The triggers can come from a variety of sources.

The triggers can come from changes in economic policy, as announced by the government and as felt through reduced tariffs, reduced excise duties, increased competition, changed bank rates, etc. Triggers can come from the level of industry competition as felt through the shift of consumer loyalty and pressures or possibilities on pricing. Suddenly, you may find your old and loyal customers dropping you. In fact, it is more likely that this would not be sudden; it is just that they have been avoiding you for a while, but you were too complacent to notice it before.

Naturally, these triggers vary from industry to industry. For instance, the cement industry experienced a huge capacity build-up in the early Nineties, while the textile machinery industry witnessed reduction in capacity around the same time. The managers of the cement companies either got different triggers or they interpreted the same events differently.

Finally, the behaviour of the economy as reflected in rise or fall in aggregate demand would act as the third set of triggers.

Not all corporate firms interpret and respond to the changes in the same manner. We suggest that some of the intervening variables could be: *continuity in extant management, management objectives, values and style of the management, financial muscle and reserve logistical strengths thought to be at their command, organisational dynamic and constraints it experiences (in matters not covered in this shortlist).* For instance, a management of a company 'belonging to' a long, established business family may have developed an ethos of placid, almost phlegmatic complacence. In addition, there may be layers of ageing family members of great or, perhaps, just greatly valued wisdom who can neither be retired nor put to any use. The young CEO who detects triggers from outside and wishes to act upon them, may have to manage this flabby and, perhaps, fairly ornamental hierarchy of grey heads before he can do so. The company's response to external changes could be shaped by that ethos. On the other hand, a fire-in-the-belly entrepreneur would respond very differently to the very same external triggers. An organisation that has had a history of severe industrial relations problems, before it underwent changes in the external environment; is bound to look at things differently than the other, whose employees are extremely cooperative.

The behaviour of the corporate firm is revealed in the form of its decisions and actions on a myriad front. Some of these can be: *introduction of new products, repositioning of existing products, changes in capacity, technology of production or logistics of production, storage and transport etc, changes in personnel policy, organisation structure, etc.* Each individual decision could be traced to a micro-decision situation, wherein it was taken. From the totality of these myriad decisions, one may be able to discern a pattern of the behavioural response of the corporate firm to the triggers it has experienced.

Finally, the consequences of the behavioural changes would naturally depend on their timing, moves of the competitors and the behaviour of the demand and supply in the ever-changing economic scenario. Thus, what the company does is important but so are some other things that it does not control—this model is shown in Figure 1.1. While the reactive-proactive continuum may be useful in understanding and perhaps even predicting business behaviour, I think it is necessary to explore how the eventual behaviour does measure up to the strategic-opportunistic dimension. As hinted at, the psychological and social determinants of behaviour and choices inherent in the decisions, implicit in the model, are of crucial importance and we shall attempt to explore them.

Figure 1.1: Triggers, variables and consequences

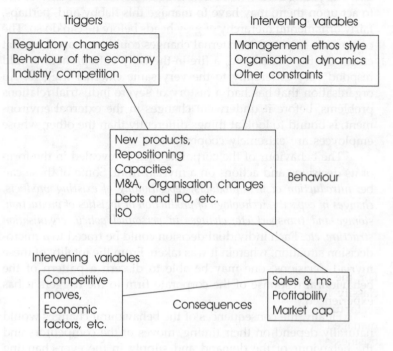

Chapter Two

THE ETHOS OF INDIAN BUSINESS HOUSES

For the purpose of discussing the ethos of Indian business, I classify Indian business in five segments. These are: the public sector units, the multinational companies, the 'business-family-managed businesses', the 'non-business family entrepreneur run businesses' and the other small business enterprises.

a) *The Public Sector Units (PSU) of the Central and the State governments.* These enterprises were set up either under the Companies Act (e.g., scores of companies like BHEL, NTPC or units in the State sector such as MELTRON, etc.) or through special Acts of the Parliament (e.g., LIC, NDDB, etc.). The Government of India (GoI) fully owns the latter category. GoI or one of the State governments owns a controlling stake in most of the enterprises in the second class. These companies do have their own governance structures in compliance of the Companies Act. Typically these companies are administered through the parent ministry through their formal boards. A lot of their procedures are defined through agencies like the Standing Committee on Public Enterprises (SCOPE). The centrally owned enterprises are subject to periodic 'enquiries' by the parliamentary committee on public undertakings, and these enquiries result in a COPU reports submitted to the parliament.

b) *The multinational companies (MNC).* By these, I refer to the subsidiaries of a company registered outside India and, perhaps, operating in more than one country. Many of them had a minority MNC stake under the FERA regime; but post liberalisation, they tended to have a majority stake owned by companies abroad.

c) *The business family managed businesses.* This category comprises of companies that belong to 'large business houses' (LBH), or may be somewhat smaller 'business families'. The term, 'large business house' was used by the MRTP Act and, in common parlance, refers to one of the bigger 'business houses'—such as Tata, Birla, Goenka, Singhania, Murugappa, Jhunjhunwala, Mahendra, Bajaj and the like. The less formidable business families are, again, old and established ones—the size of whose businesses may not be as large as that of LBH businesses. These could include Kirloskar, Nanda, Mafatlal, Sarabhai, etc.

d) *The non-business family entrepreneur run businesses.* This category comprises of the companies that are set up, owned and run by persons who do not belong to the 'business families' as categorised above. These could be companies set up by first generation entrepreneurs or by a team of people jointly taking on entrepreneurship. Reliance started in this category and may, perhaps, be moving to category 'b'. There are numerous and very illustrious examples of this kind: Gujarat Ambuja Cement, Infosys, Satyam, Dr Reddy's, Sun Pharmaceuticals, Biocon and the like.

e) *Other small business enterprises.* This category covers the huge number of tiny and small business units in organised, semi-organised or unorganised sectors. It also comprises millions of small and tiny business units run by individuals who seek to earn their livelihoods.

This categorisation is provisional; I make it essentially to understand categories more easily. Clearly, in the dynamic world of today, a specific business may shift from one category to another in a matter of weeks. The multinational, Union Carbide, for instance, sold its battery unit to Khetan; and the business shifted from category 'b' to category 'c'. Reverse shifts also occur: Kirloskar Cummins shifted from category 'c' to category 'b' sometime ago. *Thums Up* went from category 'd' to 'b', and so on. The purpose of making these categories is the belief that the pattern of business behaviour is likely to be shared within a category, and is significantly different across categories. This itself is an interesting hypothesis to test—but we shall not take it head-on, although some of our evidence, to be discussed below, does seem to indicate a degree of merit in this belief. A comprehensive examination, of how strategic or opportunistic behaviour prevails in Indian business, ought to take a comprehensive look at all these five segments. I am not going to do so. I shall attempt to build plausible enough descriptions of how a typical business firm in any of these categories behaves.

Let us start with the first category. Devoting too much attention to the problem of the public sector is unproductive for our purpose. As is commonly known, the locus of decision-making in critical business areas (such as how to adapt to a change) in a public sector seldom resides fully in these units per se. Surely there are adequate examples of how an exceptional PSU chief, manages to steer his unit in one direction or the other. But the same story about such performance is also replete with the amount of time he has to spend with his parent ministry, with the COPU people, (earlier also with the Planning Commission), the trouble he has had in doing things his way, etc. The locus of decision-making resides partially in the permanent bureaucracy of the parent ministry of the PSU in question and very significantly in the ever-changing and unpredictable political arena. Just as an example—for most of the PSU—a strategic decision to privatise has been a subject matter of political debates and wrangling, parliamentary processes and even judicial pronouncements. But the persons in the management of these units in question have largely remained somewhat perplexed and passive observers of the whole process. While a PSU like BSNL does occasionally use its position as an incumbent to profit from favourable regulatory decisions (witness the decision on Access Deficit Charges announced in October 2003), I would think it somewhat hard to argue that PSUs tend to behave opportunistically. However, I deem it best to avoid further discussion on opportunism versus strategic behaviour in the public sector units.

The discussion on 'global vs local' in Chapter one has already touched upon the difficulty of viewing the behaviour of an MNC arm in India. In the first place, the locus of decision-making regarding these businesses often resides outside India. Second, the decisions often seem to be taken based on global rather than national developments and objectives of the parent, rather than of the local arm of the MNC. I choose to ignore this category of MNC businesses too. Thus, I mainly focus on the three remaining categories: the business owned or, at any rate, run by the LBH or the less formidable business families, the businesses run by entrepreneurs who do not belong to any such family and the huge populace of the small business units in the economy.

Whether judged by the proportion of the total number of joint stock companies, share in the total volume of goods traded or representation in the largest business organisations, there is no question that the business units in category 'c' dominate in the Indian economy. For the sake of convenience I shall call these, the 'family-managed companies'. Their significance is domineering in Indian business. One has to only quickly run through some of the books or articles on this subject, to recognise this fact. For instance, Datta[1] states that almost 99 per cent of all registered companies in 1993 came from this section of business. He states (on page 30 of his book) that, of the 297000 companies with a total paid up capital of Rs 100000 crores, barely 3000 came from non-family business. In 1998, the journal, *Business India* (BI) lamented that the number of family-managed companies in the list of 'top 100 BI companies' had reduced significantly.[2] But despite that drop, the number of family business in the top 100 BI companies was around 60.

The dominance of the family-managed companies varies across product categories. Overall 'top of the mind' recall for the products reveals that about half the products are from family-managed companies. Datta also mentions that family-managed companies have weaker presence in fast moving consumer goods compared to some other products.[3] While others have lamented that family-managed business is fast becoming irrelevant to both,

[1] Datta, Sudipta; *Family Business in India*, Response Books, 1996.

[2] Radhakrishnan, N, and Dutta, Sudipta; 'Despair and Hope', *Business India*, 9 March 1998.

the consumer and the investor,[4] there is no question that it continues to be a very important segment of the Indian business, at the moment. In fact, it is so dominant and ubiquitous that one may almost equate it with usual Indian organised business; treating the non-family business as the outlier.

The domination by the family-managed business appears to be a continuation of history. As Lalita Iyer writes, 'family owned and managed business were the most common form of business organisations that managed the commerce of the Indian Ocean region, circa 1600 AD.' A single family trading in this region could handle all the stages of manufacturing and trade in a particular line. These families conducted the trade for the reasons of *dharma* as well as livelihood. Leading business families based in ports owned ships, managed trade and contracted for supplies from/ to the hinterland. Scions of the family would travel to other parts, establish business there, make a fortune and come back. Business was done in a network and through it. A network of buyers and supplier chains remained in operation for several generations. Given the primitive technology, slow communication and political uncertainty, business risks were generally high. Well-understood codes of conduct, largely based on trust, governed the trade. Business families came from well-knit communities. Many communities functioned within an established code of conducting business. They maintained elaborate accounts, usually on cash-accrual basis in single entry, bookkeeping format. While personal lifestyles were frugal, elaborate charities, ostentatious housing and lavish spending on social functions like marriages were the norms. Sharp practices were well known, and traders often used opportunities to make a quick buck.[5]

Three views, namely basically a weak entrepreneurial drive, absence of a conducive work ethic and highly frozen business traditions confined to specific caste groups, have tended to influence thinking on the Indian business ethos. Tripathi and Mehta[6] deal with these three strands of argument. The first, almost implicit in the quotation from Iyer above, is that the Indian business

[3] Datta, Sudipta; op. cit, pp. 34–36.

[4] Ninan, TN; 'Chequered Past, Uncertain Future' in *Seminar*, October 1999.

[5] Iyer, Lalita; excerpts from *The Strategic Business Spiral*, pp. 43–46.

[6] Tripathi, Dwijendra, and Mehta, Makarand; *Business Houses in Western India*, Manohar, New Delhi, 1990.

remained confined to certain castes: usually the provincial equivalent of the *vaisya varna* in the *'chaturvarana vyavastha'*. This view
is not entirely mistaken. In fact, many businessmen belong to
the vaisya communities all over the country. Yet, over a period of
time, individuals from different castes have taken to business
and have done wonderfully well. Tripathi and Mehta[7] give several
examples of people coming from a range of castes: *brahmins* (e.g.,
Kirloskars), land tillers (e.g., Amins and Patels), etc. Caste, of
course, cannot explain the presence of business families of the
non-Hindu people in India. Thus, while we would find a large
number of family businesses being run by families from the *vaisya
varna* caste, there are several others too. And the difference in
caste may not necessarily bring about a difference in business
practices.

The second view arises from the remarks made by Weber
on the work ethic in India and its influence on the absence of
entrepreneurship in India. Reduced to bare bones, his contention
was that the dominant Hindu ethos was characterised by 'other-
worldly ascetics'. This ethos did not encourage wealth accumulation nor did it encourage the people to think that their destiny was
in their own hands. The objective behind the achievement of
material wealth, and the faith in being able to achieve things by
honest and hard work, were both seen as important ingredients
of the celebrated Protestant work ethic that laid the foundation in
Weber's formulation of modern capitalism. Since both were missing in Hindu philosophy, this view argues, Hindu work ethic is
unsuitable to capitalist success. We can completely overlook the
shocking ignorance of this view, aired nearly a century ago when
the western world was croaking under the white man's burden.
It is based on insufficient information and, perhaps, suffers from
colonial snobbery.

The third view that has shaped thinking on Indian entrepreneurship is based on McClelland's 'n-ach' theory. This view, too,
makes a somewhat pessimistic prognostication about Indian business. The basic argument was that successful entrepreneurs have
a high need for achievement, or n-ach. Conversely, societies in
which most individuals have low n-ach, cannot produce great

---

[7] Tripathi, Dwijendra; and Mehta, Makarand; op. cit.

entrepreneurs. McClelland and his colleagues did cross-cultural studies to show the level of achievement motivation in different societies. They found that the n-ach level in India was low and concluded about Indian entrepreneurship pessimistically.

Aside from Indian scholars, several studies elsewhere too point out that such frozen cultural or structural explanation of entrepreneurship or business behaviour cannot be taken as valid.[8] The argument of Tripathy and Mehta is that the 'roots of entrepreneurial dynamics'—variation and commonalties in occupational choices and strategic decisions—should be found in socio-economic realities, rather than in spiritual dispensation or the baggage of cultural tradition. Even if the Hindu spiritual dispensation was rich with other worldly and ascetic values, such dictates tend to be reinterpreted by successive generations of people, and in the light of the socio-political and institutional environment as it evolves. A great deal of churning in the institutional environment perhaps occurred during the colonial rule. The conclusion seems inescapable: this colonial rule unwittingly stirred the soil of institutional arrangements, necessary for the seeds of industrial entrepreneurship to germinate. 'History must give even the devil its due!'[9]

The colonial rule saw establishment of a significant number of largely trading enterprises owned and controlled by foreigners as well as Indian business families. The foundation of family businesses of Tata, Birla and several other groups was laid during pre-Independence days. While close identification of business lines with familial background is a shade risky; one may offer a stereotype that Indian families generally tended to focus on textiles and commodity businesses, while engineering and businesses involving similar 'advanced' technologies were in foreign hands. Indeed, the family-managed companies seem to have expanded and increased their influence after Independence. During the time when India became independent, 58 of the 127 largest business companies were in British or other foreign hands. Some others were owned by foreigners, but managed by Indian agents. Companies owned and managed by Indians, were about 40. Explicit

[8] Ruttan, M; 'A historical and comparative view on the studies of Indian Entrepreneurship', *Economic Sociology*, 3:2, February 2002.

[9] Tripathi, Dwijendra, and Mehta, Makarand; op. cit, pp. 185–97.

efforts to reduce concentration of economic power in the hands of a few were initiated in the sixties and culminated in making of the MRTP Act. While the state sector focused on creation of public sector enterprises in the 'key critical' areas of economy and the heavy industry segments, multinationals experienced an increasingly hostile regime. In some sense, this was even more hostile to them than to the class of family-managed companies. The multinationals were doubly doomed: they represented the ugly face of foreign capitalism and, of course, held a near-monopolistic sway in their respective segments. In general, the multinational companies were less dexterous in managing the governments. In consequence, the class of family-managed companies kept growing in importance. By 1995, 80 per cent of the top 500 companies were from the family-managed groups. This rise has happened despite an explicitly anti-business family approach of the successive governments.[10]

As Tripathi[11] says, 'three factors may account for the remarkable resilience that the family business has demonstrated in free India.' They are:

- *The family holdings in companies, although much lower than during the pre-Independence days, are still sufficient to ensure that the family cannot be easily displaced from the management.* The investing class is now considerably expanded in response to more vibrant stock markets. As a result, shareholdings in the companies have become more widely disbursed than even before. The amorphous group of individual investors cannot pose any real threat to the family supremacy. The financial institutions, with their large shareholdings, can do so but they have obviously considered it more prudent to stand by the existing managements.
- *The post-Independence leadership in most business families has been in competent hands; capable of leading their managerial workforce from the front, and evoking a great deal of trust from the shareholders in their companies.* While only a few of the leading lights of the private corporate sector before Independence could boast of high levels of education or

---

[10] Datta, Sudipta; op. cit, pp. 24–30.
[11] Tripathi, Dwijendra; 'Change and Continuity', *Seminar*, October 1999.

professional training, their successors are well-educated and well-versed in the art of management. So are the leaders of the new business families that have sprung up in recent years. The younger generations may or may not have the vision and entrepreneurial traits of their fathers, but with their managerial capabilities and technical skills they have been able to introduce a certain measure of professionalism in the management of their companies.

Until very recently, the private sector firms have been operating in a protected atmosphere. Though constrained by the licence-permit dispensation, they had an almost undisputed sway over a large domestic market. Their products admittedly were shoddy and services poor by world standards, but the virtual absence of competition from superior quality goods helped most of the companies offer good returns on investment. The investors, therefore, had little reason to feel dissatisfied with the management. Firms in unprotected sectors such as textiles did suffer, but this caused no irreparable damage to the standing of most of the prominent families, as they had highly diversified portfolios.

Lastly, there has been no tradition of corporate raiding in India, matters like the takeover trade are of much more recent origin.

I offer a rough and ready summary of the evolution and social reality of Indian business, drawn from the works referred above as also others, before taking up the more important issues for detailed discussion.

a) *Indian family-managed business is substantially of mercantile-capitalist origin.* The trader-cum-money lender of yester-years is the forefather of a large number of businesses. He comes from the *marwari, parsi, bohra, bania, lala, kayasth, chettiar, vani* or other such castes in different regions of the country. As noted earlier, this association of business with mercantile capitalism should not be interpreted as an absolute association between business and castes. Its implications are more to do with business attitudes than with family roots.

b) *Indian business tradition arose in the context of two features.* On the one hand, crafts and artisans were plentiful and largely met the demand of a dominantly rural populace. Honey-comb-like replication of almost identical craftsmen enter-prises, perhaps also linked by kinship, provided the bulk of the base for our production logistics. This was not so different from the pre-industrial revolution in Europe or China. Except that, in India, it got inexorably mixed with the caste system in India. The celebrated *vishwakarma* castes became the original forerunners of workshops and other production facilities. The second feature was the emergence and entrenchment of powerful kinship networks of traders and money managers, as noted above by Iyer.

c) *In case of both, the artisan/craftsmen and the trader-cum-money-lenders, business and family affairs were quite inexorably linked.* The family culture and tradition is quite elaborate in these matters. The business power remains in male hands, and passes on from the father to the eldest son, and so on. There, of course, are exceptions and these rules are not frozen. Point is that, the status in the family and the status in the business are never de-linked from each other. The inexo-rable link between family and the business continues till this date. This has carried itself into the modern family busi-nesses in India. Such links may take unexpected forms. For instance Geeta Piramal[12] states that a large business house bought a huge company for a princely sum; not because it added to its core strengths, but because 'it would be a fit occupation for its rising son!' Thus family hierarchy, family priorities, etc. are quite important in many businesses.

d) *During the servitude of a hundred odd years, much of Indian enterprise confined itself to the management of logistics of either procurement of commodities for the British companies or the distribution of such imported manufactures that were available and sold in the country.* A section of Indian businessmen and, according to Tripathi, the section that did not belong to the conventional business families, did identify opportunities in manufacturing. The *banias* and the *chettiars* confined themselves largely to trading, while new entrepreneurs took to establishments of manufacturing units. But for the dominant trading class, the instrument for both domestic

---

[12] Piramal, Geeta; *Business Maharajas*, Viking, New Delhi, 1996.

procurement and distribution of the imported goods was the management agency system prevalent till the Fifties and the early Sixties. In the war-torn years of shortages, the management agencies assumed monopoly character for the lay Indian public, while also breeding monopoly attitudes among the agents.

e) *For nearly forty years after Independence, the permit-quota-ration* raj *prevailed.* This was the era of shortages of practically everything. This made a king of the trader, a goat of the industrialist and a supplicant of the customer. Consequently, the statement 'customer is the king' tends to be viewed with shocked disbelief by many a customer ('Who, me? A king? You must be joking!'), when it comes to a large number of items and, particularly, in far-flung areas of the country. Even today, in competitive lines like seeds for crops, a lot of tribal farmers sow what their *seth* gives them, rather than choose what they want to sow!

f) *The MRTP and the logic of the Centrally planned economy made it difficult, if not impossible, for businessmen to expand business according to their own assessments.* Expansion of capacity, setting up facilities for backward or forward integration, etc. were tasks that needed a huge manoeuvre through the bureaucratic layers that controlled and throttled growth.

g) *As a result, achieving focus, reaching optimal production capacities, cost effectiveness, material use efficiency, high product quality, etc. took a backseat to successfully 'cornering' a permit for some commodity in shortage, or some scarce license.* We find a bewildering absence of focus in the range of activities of 'traditional' business firms. And, if their line is basically the same, they seem to spread horizontally rather than grow vertically.

h) *There has always been a preference in business families to give free space to each of the aspiring male to do his own thing.* This family's preference for settling each of the siblings into their own lines of business further accentuated the trend for multiple units in unrelated businesses, horizontal growth, etc. For instance, a family runs a cement dealership, owns and runs a unit for pharmaceutical formulation, has a hotel and restaurant and has a small-time construction firm—all, under one roof. Such is the case of a this-day firm in Nagpur. Thousands like it still exist.

i) *The focus of Indian business is on managing money. Products and services offered are incidental.*

j) *As Gurucharan Das*[13] *points out, 'there appear to be common weaknesses in Indian family-managed companies',* though stating them in an a peremptory manner like this may be a bit unfair to some of them. These weaknesses are:

- An inability to separate the family's interest from the interest of the business,
- A lack of focus and business strategy,
- A short-term approach to business, leading to
- An absence of investment in employees and in product development, and
- Insensitivity towards the customer.

The key issues facing the family business, as discussed by Gurucharan Das and others, include the following:

- *Product vs Commodity:* Many family-managed companies have to adapt to the changed, new world order in which they compete; on the basis of the quality of their product and not merely on the basis of their control over an item in short supply. Winning the consumer mind and retaining it, are skills they need to learn and nurture. Undoubtedly, several of them have already acquired a formidable reputation for their products: Raymond suiting, Bajaj scooters, Crompton fans and the whole range of Tata products, of course; offer such examples. Yet, many a family business, that prospered in the commodity business line, will have to change gears and mindsets.

- *Mission and Market vs Money Management:* This is what Das calls 'achieving strategic focus from a bewilderingly inexplicable diversification.' He gives the examples of how Khetan does not invest in tea, but buys a battery unit, etc. He argues that it takes painstaking efforts to master a particular technology and product; and only such mastery can lend durability to one's business. Much of the loss of place and glory of Indian family business seems to be due to this very aspect.

---

[13] Das, Gurucharan; 'The Problem' in *Seminar*, p. 482, October 1999.

Professional Management vs Control Orientation: Not too long ago, a leading doyen of Indian industry said in an interview, 'the professional manager is not loyal and cannot be trusted—in general, we need to evolve our own philosophy of management because the western theory of management is not applicable to Indian conditions.' He went on to become the president of the Federation of Indian Chamber of Commerce and Industry (FICCI). An author on family businesses has stated[14] that family-run, business houses tend to shun professionally qualified managers, while showing a distinct preference for Chartered Accountants (CA). This, says the author, is based on the perception that the latter are less aggressive and less offensive in their interpersonal relations—and are, thus, best suited to an environment where there is a premium on loyalty, rather than on professionalism. Very recently, a manager from the State Bank of India said that while their bank is spending huge amounts on some fancy management consultants, they find the latter not very relevant in dealing with the difficult situation on the ground in things like rural credit. I hear so many statements in this vein. *Ad nauseum,* I have been told by Indian businessmen that the average MBA is no good and that 'the western management theory is not applicable to Indian conditions.' Yes, the high-profile MBA, from a big-time educational institution, is said to be earning millions in the very first year of his career. Usually he earns that much in American companies which, by hiring him, can get very high quality human resource, and, perhaps, can also fulfil their self-imposed obligations as per the norms of equal opportunities. At least they also save a lot of dollars, given that a comparable East-Coast MBA in USA will cost much more. Simultaneously, the classically Indian business is still chary of trusting him. The core issue seems to be a combination of two things—a xenophobic resistance to something that is viewed as an external, alien imposition; and a personal discomfort with the aggressive, questioning and irreverent attitudes of the persons who represent it. Claiming that the western management thought is irrelevant; is how

---

[14] Datta, Sudipta; op. cit.

this distrust seems to find its expression. In fact, one of the objectives of this book is to address that question. Even a statement of dubious validity assumes a measure of truth, when repeated often. Before examining whether strategy matters at all in Indian businesses, it is necessary to outline the ethos of business in India and explore this question of validity of the management theory for Indian conditions. This chapter does so.

Indian Business and Ethics of Business

When we talk of management theory in India, I am tempted to bring in the *Bhagwat Gita*, Kautilya's *Arthashastra*, etc.; but I shall not go back to the 'Indian values as laid down in pristine texts'. While I, myself, am moderately religious, I wish to find answers to social questions like this one in social reality rather than mythological-religious preaching. I am not certain whether the code of Hindu ethics legitimised dishonesty among the traders. In his book, Sekhar[15] indirectly says so. He quotes Subramaniam to show the prevalence of particularistic values in Hindu ethics, permitting traders to cheat and deceive. (p. 23)

He also states how Hindu ethics distinguished between corruption that damages the interest of the state, and the acts of dishonesty that bring loss to other individuals. It is only that the former is called corruption and is severely looked down upon. Tilak[16] makes somewhat more ambivalent statements. He states that ethics permit prevarication in the situation when one's own property is threatened, but Hindu ethics never permit cheating or outright chicanery. The *Bhagvat Gita* just makes a reference that agriculture, animal husbandry and trade are the assigned tasks of the *vaisyas*, but makes no statement about the code of ethics regarding it *(Srimad Bhagvat Gita,* 18:44). But the reality is sordid.[17]

---

[15] Sekhar, RC; *Ethics in Business*, Response Books, New Delhi, 1997.

[16] Tilak, Bal Gangadhar; *Geeta Rahasya*, p. 64.

[17] See, for instance Ashok Advani's publisher's letter in *Business India*, 20 September 1999; in which he talks of the ubiquitous tendency of generating black money in business and how that tends to cause ruptures in families. He suggests that south Indian families do this to a much lesser extent and, hence, can survive even unto third generations.

Probity and transparency[18] are so alien to Indian business that, using today's constructs, we may even call these concepts 'cultural aggression of the west'. This explains the sullen and hunted looks on the faces of Indian business leaders, during the talks on making the Generally Accepted Accounting Principles (GAAP) or good governance, etc. mandatory. Why did it happen? Irrespective of whether Hindu religion legitimises it or otherwise, there is no doubt that the following five factors have existed for a pretty long time in modern, post-Independence India:

- The prevalence of monopolistic strength among traders and suppliers of goods and services in general, greatly rein-forced by shortages.
- Extremely high marginal rate in income tax that prevailed for a long time.
- Multiple-point taxation from multiple taxing agencies, per-mitting even more confusing set of norms for defining tax liability and granting exemptions.
- Falling standards of probity in public life.[19]
- Very slack and lenient enforcement and almost silly punish-ments, for severe economic offences. (For instance, private telephone operators were required to provide rural connec-tions. Failure to do so attracted a fine of a few lakh rupees, perhaps, while these people saved tens of crores of rupees in not doing what was their contract-bound obligation.)

In consequence, the business ethos was, and perhaps still is, not conducive to making patient, painstaking and conscientious busi-nessmen confident about their correctness. All the readers of this book are, of course, gentlemen who would rather hang themselves than do anything illegal. Yet, when one sees a large number of people making quick money by cutting corners and adopting dubious means and, still, getting away scot-free; a man feels uncomfortable, naturally. One starts wondering why one should be the patient man who must stick to the right side of the law? Had

---

[18] For some telling comments on transparency in Indian business family run corporate houses, Kaveri Mittra's article 'Remaking Duncans', *Business India*, 2 November 1998.

[19] In fact, this is common knowledge; but even so for a 'documented' support-ing point, see 'Indicting a Political Class' in *Business India*, 29 January 1996.

it just been a matter of affecting the psychology of industrialists, it would have been a different matter. But the tragedy is that it actually makes the task of running business with probity extremely difficult, often unviable.

Let us see an example, perhaps the most telling of them all. I feel quite confident about my facts here, because I once studied and wrote a book on the oilseeds industry.[20]

Box 2.1: The sordid ethos of Indian business: An illustration from the oilseeds industry

Let us look at the Indian oilseeds industry, easily among the most primitive and crude in the world. It is still very difficult, if not impossible, for a high technology, professionally managed firm to do well in the Indian oil industry. You may not believe that a public sector unit can be high-tech or professional; so, the performance of the National Dairy Development Board (NDDB) and *Dhara* may not impress you. What about ITC Agrotech (now Conagra)? Rated among those having the best techology in the Nineties, the plant has not been able to make money for over a decade. Why is that so? The reasons are in the ethos. In the first place, the rate of commercial taxes (purchase tax, *mandi* cess, sales tax and turnover tax) amounts to about 12 per cent by value of the oil, and the margins are 3–4 per cent, on an average. Tax evasion is rampant, the norm rather than exception. Tax collection as a percentage of the potential, ranges from a low of 6–7 per cent in Andhra Pradesh (AP), to a high of 60–65 per cent in Madhya Pradesh (MP). (It is high in MP because there are relatively small numbers of all regulated, registered solvent extraction plants—each of which must file so many returns. Also, because it is consolidating even now.) As a result, those who pay taxes suffer negative margins and cannot survive. Then there is the issue of massive 'adulteration'; that is, unauthorised mixing of oils (such as palm oil, cottonseed oil or soyabean oil mixed with groundnut oil) to bring down the unit cost of oil.

(contd.)

---

[20] Phansalkar, SJ; and Gulati, VP; *Oilseeds and Edible Oil Economy of India*, Vikas, New Delhi, 1994.

(Box contd.)

Since it needs specialised equipment to detect adulteration, and since most state food inspectors possess none of these, this adulteration is quite regular. In fact, unless you buy a respected brand like *Dhara* or *Sundrop*, the chances of your getting pure groundnut oil, when you pay for groundnut oil, are even smaller than the chances of people living in Kolkata getting milk that is not reconstituted from milk powder. As a result of these factors, there are real diseconomies of scale. Large players cannot remain faceless, cannot do all such dubious dealings and, hence, cannot survive. As a sad consequence, the industry is extremely fragmented with thousands of old, inefficient and hopelessly dirty processing facilities.

I am sure that if you work with or in a small and medium industry of whatever type, you are tempted to narrate how your sector of industry is worse than the oilseeds sector. However, do remember that the margins, in most sectors, are much better than 3 per cent; and that there is a huge pressure of imports in oilseeds industry.

The regulations have eased and simplified since the Nineties, leaving less scope for manipulative behaviour; and competition has, of course, increased manifold. But, mindsets do not change so quickly. The point about business ethos is not merely bemoaning the sad state of the country, but it creates a concrete issue to be tackled.

(Let us return to an aside, for a while. Do you see where the perception of irrelevance of the management theory comes in? The businessman argues, perhaps in a somewhat convoluted and less articulated manner, 'Look, all this formal and proper management is a bad idea in India. In the first place, with slack regulations, you can make more money by managing your tax matters smartly, by managing all these government fellows and by sticking to things that give quick returns; than by making better products. After all, why make a better product when whatever you make can sell— albeit at a lower price,[21] when the consumer has no redressal, and

---

[21] The biographer of a leading Indian businessman wryly commented in an essay he wrote after the businessman's death, about the quality consciousness in

the law enforcement is so slack? And, then, no one pays a premium for quality anyway. Also, see how everyone is entering into all sorts of businesses. Yesterday's polyster textile mill becomes a software firm in half-a-year; talking about B2B and B2C, like an expert. So who told you all this about focus, synergy, common thread, experience curve and the rest of it? As long as you control cash flow, and enter a line when the chances for entry are good, you are home. All the formal theory is bunk.' Do you see their point? Do you agree?

My submission is threefold. In the first place let us separate the seamy side of things from hard business issues of product mix, extent of focus, etc. If one is focused on a single line and develops expertise in it, one will be able to make a better, cheaper product and, perhaps, expand volumes and variety too. For making money, white or black, your products must sell—is it not so? Theoretically, the better your product, the better it can sell. One may still play monkey with the law and make more money than the next-door unit that only plays with the law, without developing expertise in the product. (For the record, let me clearly state that I do not recommend playing monkey with the law; even selectively, as some recent Gurus have recommended!) Thus most of the 'good general management' we talk about, is basically valid for Indian circumstances as well.

Second, the fundamental question is, 'what is the main objective of the entrepreneur?' If it is to make a pile as quickly as possible, why should we be the sourpusses who pout at him? If he can do so playing monkey with the law; well, good luck to him. He is of no interest to us. An entrepreneur who desires to become big as an industrialist, and a business that becomes a global player are of interest to us. For such a man, facelessness is counter-productive. Attributes of reliability, dependability, solidity, respectability and probity—all, kind of hang together. Shifty, too-smart-by-half and sharp-shooting behaviour is associated with a unit that cannot be trusted as far you can throw an elephant. Hence, the entrepreneur must avoid these 'smart' tricks to the

---

the latter's group. He stated that the family insisted on sending an empty car to accompany the one that was taking the biographer on his travels, just in case. Both cars were products of a company belonging to the businessman and the family was simply not sure about its cars.

extent he can, not on moral grounds (and there is nothing shameful about being moral!) but on grounds of far sightedness. As Ninan[22] points out, the old ways of acquiring promoter capital have also become more problematic. Then, all that you needed to do was cream off 10 per cent or more, from the capital cost of your project, recycle it as the promoter's equity contribution, and build even further capital by creaming off through sole selling arrangements and the like. But in today's world of pesky equity analysts who respect nobody, none of this helps. Markets are too competitive for transferring sales commissions into private pockets, because it costs you in price competitiveness. Business valuation suffers, and the competitive edge is lost. Now, the game is gaining the trust of the investor. Winning it is difficult enough; winning it after it was lost earlier is doubly so. If, at the same time, the financial institutions are beginning to ask questions, if talk of corporate governance is in the air, and if raising fresh capital becomes even more difficult in the new environment; the 75 families can survive as significant business entities, only by changing the way they do business.

The Nineties

A recent book[23] has stated that they found that there was ubiquitous prevalence of satisfactory underperformance in Indian business. The authors suggest that even when firms are able to articulate what they consider to be criteria for satisfactory performance in sharp business terms; so much sales growth per annum and so much return on capital invested, for instance; it is amazingly common to find senior executives, including their owners, to be complacent and satisfied even when the firm is not achieving the stated threshold level of performance. They attribute this to the presence of external arrogance and internal control orientation in most firms. This arises due to a pattern of early success in managing protecting competition, achieving initial growth and profits leading to a spurious belief in one being the best. It then

---

[22] Ninan, TN; op. cit.

[23] Ghoshal, Sumantra and Piramal, Gita and Bartlett, C; In particular, see pages 8–15, *Managing Radical Change*, Penguin, New Delhi, 2000.

combines with the overall feudal, social order in creating a flabby management structure with too many people not doing too much. The success leads to external arrogance, and batteries of redundant staff lead to internal control orientation. The tragedy is that this combination often leads to complacency, stifling of innovation and initiative and then into the morass of satisfactory underperformance.

I believe that Ghoshal *et al*, have been far more charitable to Indian business than they need to be. They ignore, perhaps deliberately, the ugly reality that for at least two and a half decades since 1965, the dominant objective of a large proportion of Indian business had only incidental relationship with formal business performance. Extremely high rates of taxation, progressively worsening standards of ethics in political and administrative rungs of regulatory and enforcement arms of the state, weak regulation and slack enforcement permitted full freedom to the base instinct of greed for easy money to grow. Crony capitalism, complete absence of transparency in governance and the hapless state of the small investor left unguarded by regulators allowed private sector corruption and black money generation to grow to an unprecedented scale. How does one otherwise explain the executives of a BIFR company living in opulent luxury, such as buying a helicopter for movement within Mumbai? How does one explain that the reported level of coffee exports from India were 10 times as much as the volumes that were reported to have actually been received in importing ports? While refreshing in its rare candour, Advani's letter, quoted above, really reveals no well-guarded secret. Piramal[24] mentions in her book that a star of a large business house had to constantly spend time sorting out fights and squabbles within his clan, as the clan had huge and complex control over extremely large properties and assets. She makes a disingenuous statement that even the income tax department would not know how much the clan really owned. I quite definitely believe that this assumed ignorance of the income tax people was wholly correct but did not reflect their incompetence. The ignorance was, perhaps, soothingly nurtured to kill all curiosity about the reality. For a significant part of Indian business, the generation of unaccounted personal wealth of the 'promoters' was

---

[24] Piramal, Gita; op. cit, p. 135 onwards.

the central if not the primary goal of businesses, while formal business performance was an unavoidable nuisance. This was more so, since businesses preferred financing their plans through huge chunks of equity placed with government financial institutions, along with even larger debts from them. They never felt the need for rewarding the shareholders at all. Perhaps the first major break from this trend came with the Ambanis who, after being rebuffed by public financial institutions, decided to raise finances through public and, hence, chose to reward the shareholders.[25] For most other businesses, the gain and the wealth of the 'non-family' shareholder were, at best, a matter of idle curiosity. Thus, businesses were run to make money basically for the promoters; and many of them were deliberately and blithely colour-blind. If the objectives of the business were not about achieving formal business growth for a long time, how do Ghoshal et al expect the business executives to be overly concerned about them? Was the complacency about listless, formal performance not scripted in the way business was done? And if the ethos was this way for 30 years, why should anyone change too dramatically in only a few years into the Nineties?

What happened in reality is, of course, history. As a noted commentators put it, 'In a country where the family is still the basic unit of management in most businesses, the past 20 years will not be remembered very fondly. The traditional family enterprises were the biggest casualty in the steadily accelerating process of re-organisation that has been taking place through much of corporate India. While on the one hand, business houses have had to split their assets, often destructively, to take care of the emerging new family environment; on the other hand, they have had to deal with new economic realities—increasing domestic competition in the 1980s and international competition in the 1990s. So it is not surprising that at least one-third of the names on the list of top 100 of 1978, do not feature in the 1997 Business India Super 100 list. Many companies have just disappeared without a trace.'[26]

Businesses did not behave in a very unexpected manner. There was a lot of effort in refocusing or enhancing focus on core

---

[25] Piramal, Gita; op. cit, pp. 5–8.

[26] Radhakrishnan, N; and Dutta, Sudipta; 'Despair and Hope', Business India, 9 March 1998.

line of business.[27] Some tried cost cutting.[28] The need for downsizing had been recognised by many, but labour legislation did not permit it till quite sometime after the liberalisation process started. Downsizing—or to be more fashionable—rightsizing was done in a large number of companies, and is still going on.[29]

Major Issues

However, there are two important issues that observers throw up about Indian business and the way it responded to changes in the environment. The first is the troublesome problem of unrelated diversification in an extremely large number of businesses. The most commonly known and commented upon case is of the Ruiyas, who tried several unrelated diversifications: iron pellets, oil refining and telecom. The story of drug makers venturing into GSM telephony is well known. But the phenomenon is not restricted to these high profile business houses alone. BI has commented upon at least 10 such instances, as shown in Box 2.2.

Then there are other 'funny' diversifications: Deccan Cements going in for polyster filament yarn and, hence, setting up DCL Polysters; Dr Reddy's setting up a unit to make halogen lamps, a scion of the Birlas setting up a furniture marketing arm, Nav Bharat group of publications, in central India, setting up a teak plantations company; and so on. Usually—but not always—what seems to happen is that the decision to make such a diversification is taken when the company has surplus investible money, and an opportunity seems attractive. Almost with the same frequency, most such unrelated diversifications bomb—at least if one looks at formal business performance as the sole deciding criteria. So rampant is the phenomenon that its explanation is really necessary, and five strands of explanations are offered by observers:[30]

---

[27] For instance, articles on TVS, *Business India*, 23 February 1995; Jindals, *Business India*, 3 July 1995; and Kanorias, *Business India*, 6 November 1995.

[28] For instance, Mysore Kirloskar, 'A Quick Recovery', *Business India*, 16 December 1995.

[29] This is far too common a phenomenon now, and does not need much support of articles or papers. For instance, 'Spinning out of Danger', *Business India*, 1 June 1998.

[30] I thank my friends, Sarvashri Sriram, MS; Laddha, Sham B and Bhagvat, Ramesh; for contributing to the ideas presented here.

Box 2.2: Indian business and the way it responded to changes in the environment

S. no.	Company	Core line	Intended or implemented unrelated diversification	Reference to *BI* article dated
1	NIIT	IT training	Telecom	27 February 1995
2	Coromondel Fertilizers	Fertilizers	Cement	5 June 1995
3	Chitale group	Milk, food products	Glazed tiles	1 January 1996
4	Aruna Sugar	Sugar	Hotels, leather	1 January 1996
5	Unitech	Construction	Aquaculture	3 June 1996
6	SCICI	Shipping finance	Insurance	12 August 1996
7	Kinetic Motors	Two wheelers	High speed elevators	24 February 1997
8	Lakshmi Machine Works (LMW)	Textile machines	Granite, Floriculture, Palm oil	7 April 1997
9	Piramals	Pharma	Shopping malls	23 August 1999
10	Himatsignka Seide	Textile	Building and Real estate	2 February 1999

Source: Business India.

(i) *Legacy of the past*. In the managing agency era (after the time the country became independent and before managing agencies were disallowed), a fair number of business families had worked as managing agents for ex-patriate businessmen. Managing agencies looked after really diverse business—usually trading, tea/coffee estates and very elementary manufacturing businesses of the patrons. They managed amazingly diverse lines for different patrons. As such, most business houses that achieved any stature later; were diversified from the very start. The concept of unrelated diversification really did not jar on them; in fact, it was almost as natural to them as any other, ordinary business practice. The technical core of a business was to be handled by a technocrat, and the rest was basically the management of money and trade which the family or its trusted men did. This legacy persists at least in the mindset of the businessmen from these families. So, unrelated diversifications are very common. The second legacy of the past is about regulation. In the Centrally planned economy, where the implementation of the MRTP Act was a politically sensitive issue, it was neither easy nor possible to expand and consolidate one's position in a particular product line. Hence, a businessman who had earned profits in one line and wished to invest; was almost forced to go into another line. Some extraordinary and visionary businessmen managed to grow in one line by adopting a range of tricks and strategies, but the ordinary businessman preferred to start another line and save himself the bother. This facet, repeated several times over, made unrelated diversification more or less the expected and accepted pattern of growth.

(ii) *The second contributing factor has been the ubiquitous desire of all businessmen to ensure that his children did not step onto each other's feet.* So he sets up businesses that have only the working capital as the common thread; and gives each of his sons, one business to manage. This proliferation of essentially small businesses is quite different from the proliferation of dummy firms that I mention as blunder number five in my earlier book.[31] The latter proliferation of dummy

---

[31] Phansalkar, SJ; *How Not to Ruin Your Small Industry*, Response Books, pp. 70–74, 1996.

firms is intended to save on taxes or on expenses required under a variety of regulations in force. Here, the proliferation occurs simply to ensure that the siblings have their own free space to grow. When the sons have such freedom, the chances of the family staying united are believed to improve. (Of course, as Advani mentions in the letter quoted above, this unity can be fractured because of hassles of distribution of black money, but leave that for the moment) Hence, while one brother manages a large two-wheelers' business, the other deals with electrical goods, and so on. The Ambanis offered what is among rare exceptions to this general pattern; yet, one wonders whether the size and scope of the *Reliance Infocomm* business was planned with a similar objective in mind?

(iii) *The third contributing factor is a common trait, of the sons not wanting to do what their father did or is doing.* This trait was missing in the earlier times, because the business was hopelessly interlinked with family affairs, because most elder sons never got the opportunity to study, observe and learn different things as they were drawn in the parent's business at a very early age; and because businesses never involved more than 'proper behaviour with *biradari*' of the businessmen of the clan. But since the last 50 years or so, most affluent businessmen have been sending their children to study abroad. Now the number of MBAs from the Harvard, Wharton, Stanford or Michigan business schools in traditional business families; perhaps exceeds a few hundred. These boys are definitely the suit-and-tie people, and no more the *dhoti*-clad type. They simply do not want to get into the 'same old rut', which is being managed by the *dhotiwalas* anyway. Besides, the clan sort of frowns if the son is absorbed in the father's business. The son gets branded as being mediocre, almost incompetent, as to have required the father to 'accommodate' him in his own business. The expectation of the clan and the self-perception of the son, both, work in the same direction; and the son ends up starting a new business, often unrelated to the old line. Some first-rate business growth has come about due to this pattern, as is shown by the example of WIPRO. Yet, the fact is also that a lot of unrelated diversification has come about this way.

(iv) *Associated with this is the feeling that value migration will make the firm more attractive.* This can happen if, for good reasons, the management feels that the existing business line is no longer attractive—either in terms of profit margins or in terms of sales growth—because of the limitations of the market size or the onset of fierce MNC competition, or whatever other reason. And if it believes that the new line that it has spotted, offers far better value for the investment. In such an event, the decision to diversify in the new line—however unrelated it may seem—would be justified for reasons of value migration, to enhance the sustainability of the firm. There are a few examples of this type. It is possible that, by taking a shot at telecom, the tractor maker attempted value migration of this type. However, this would turn out to be a spacious argument if it is seen that the focal company is indulging in numerous and unrelated diversifications—as is suggested by the example of LMW (Box 2.2). However, some of the seemingly unrelated and 'funny' diversifications can be attributed to value migrations.

(v) *The most common observation made by people is that companies, like individuals, succumb to the temptations of the bubble of the day.* If one looks at the last two decades, there have been several such bubbles. The CTV boom at first, and then the lease finance boom were, both, seen in the Eighties. These attracted the very best and the brightest in their charming vortex. Then there was the dairy bubble in the early Nineties, when a reputed builder and a steel mill—among others—were attracted to it. Then came the granite bubble, followed by the software bubble with its Y2K appeal. More recently, there have been the telecom and the insurance bubbles. I have already commented upon entrants in the telecom line; those in Insurance are, apparently, even more 'funny': Dabur, Bajaj, IFFCO group and so many others; whose lines were not financial services, and have got into insurance. Bajaj, of course, had huge cash reserves and a long-standing treasury wing; but some of the others did not. Of late, two more bubbles are still doing the rounds: chain retailing, by setting up huge shopping malls, and BPO. Whether value migration explains it, whether it is the temptation and the dream of becoming a big financial company, or whether it is sheer opportunism—is a matter of post mortem and interpretation. Basically, what I suggest is that quite a few of these unrelated diversifications are effected when the company has surplus cash, and has been led to believe that the particular line is a 'hot' thing.

The second problem, as Ghoshal[32] et al put it, is the near-ubiquitous tendency of incrementalism in decision-making. They state that most managers in Indian businesses were brought up in an era of crippling regulations, infrastructure bottlenecks, and the dominance of bureaucracy and poor systems. In such an era, it was possible to make only incremental changes. This ethos made meant that the tenets of this religion called 'incrementalism' were valid. Strategic thinking and decision-making often requires thinking big, new and bold. The crippling constraints posed by the ethos made this very difficult. Reliance offers a more or less unique exception; in that the company thought big despite the constraints and the odds, found new ways of doing things (such as accessing relatively cheap and sure-shot capital from the ordinary investor by ensuring that he was rewarded constantly) and worked hard for changing the crippling constraints. As Piramal remarks in her book, Reliance certainly obtained several favourable policy shifts and worked very hard to complete huge projects right in time that made their credibility soar with the investors, with the market and with the government. Most other businesses were more conservative and opted for incrementalism. This is not to say that there were no instances of meteoric growth, or of truly breathtakingly bold decisions of a strategic nature. Several examples of this kind can be cited. Some made it big before they went bust, others succeeded. One may put the giddy pace of expansion at Core in this category. Core went bust and headed towards BIFR—perhaps owing to reasons of 'becoming over-ambitious about a product category (IV fluids) that was known to have a limited market', as one pharma observer put it. In the same bracket, one may also include the example of Dr Reddy setting up an R&D facility to develop its own molecules at a cost that almost equalled its turnover in the early Nineties in this

---

[32] Ghoshal, Sumantra et. al; op. cit, p. 14.

bracket. This surely paid off in a decade, when Dr Reddy became a leading contender of original products, even as it reaped the advantages of reverse engineering and the process patent regime in India.

But a middle path—of thinking big and proceeding incrementally—is perhaps more commonly observed in India, and seems to yield greater chance of success. One may consider Tata's relentless pursuit of the passenger car market, until it attained success in this category. They moved through phases: from manufacturing only trucks to being a manufacturer of utility vehicles, then moving on to the manufacture of passenger cars using facilities known to them, and then to making the *Indica*—till they reached a stage where the change of name suggests a larger focus on cars, relegating the truck line to the background. Amul's transformation from being an ideologically oriented 'basic needs' type of dairy, to one that competes with the best and the brightest for the real big money in ice creams, and now in beverages; is perhaps of this ilk. The most current example of a decision that contributes towards making the crippling constraints largely incidental; is that of the famous *e-chaupals* of ITC. Yet, their development as well as implementation is classically incremental and conservative—reminding one of the McKinsey mantra of three horizons (embryonic, emergent and mature).

Let me sum up the observations, writings and comments of other scholars on Indian business. There is a general agreement that a great deal of Indian business is still dominated by the family. There is a plethora of comments about what this entails: absence of transparency, distrust of professional managers, focus on management of money rather than missions or markets; prevalence of hiatus between operative objectives of the dominant management group and the formal business objectives that get stated, difficulties of keeping the flock together due to inherent problems of equitable distribution of spoils, etc. Then there is a well-argued case for the prevalence of acceptance of satisfactory underperformance; which may or may not have been caused by the hiatus between operative goals and business goals. In reality, commentators have noted that Indian business behaves much the way one would expect it to: repositioning products, cost cutting, rightsizing, refocusing, etc. There is a bewildering and continuing occurrence of unrelated diversification that could be caused by some of the family related factors, or by preference of value migration; but is more likely the result of opportunism, gullibility to current bubbles and a desire for a quick return. Finally, there is the comment about the religion of incrementalism. While we see examples of big and bold thinking, we see that path to be somewhat strewn with failed ventures. What seems to suit the Indian temper is, to think big and act incrementally.

Chapter Three

UNDERSTANDING BUSINESS STRATEGY IN THE INDIAN CONTEXT

This chapter is devoted to the discussion of concepts and constructs, necessary to understand a business and how it responds to changes around it. I am quite aware that to most readers trained in business, this chapter will be superfluous. However, I believe that it will only be partially so. This chapter will serve the purpose of a 'ready reckoner' for those who have studied business. And it will serve the purpose of defining and clarifying the terms used, for those who are not formally trained in business. As the title of this book suggests, I am concerned with the relevance of strategic business in the Indian context. It is incumbent upon me to specify what I mean by strategic behaviour. This is what I set out to do in the first part of this chapter. In the second part, I try to look at various constructs that help us understand how businesses respond to the changes in their environment. I start with a brief discussion of natural competition as opposed to strategic competition, and then address the issue of business strategy.

Natural and Strategic Competition

Whenever there are more claimants or demand-makers for a resource than what the resource base can supply, competition is the result. In nature, flora and fauna compete for nutrients, water and sunlight. They compete for survival. Other than human beings, few species indulge in hoarding—they only take what they need. Some may instinctively 'save' for a rainy day, but very few indulge in mindless stockpiling. Thus, the main competition is for mere survival. Such competition occurs at two stages: In the first place, when different species compete with each other for a set of resources that sustain them; and, second, when individual members of the same species compete with each other for survival. The first type of competition—the competition between species—occurs over generations. Biologists tell us that species differentiate among themselves and develop, through natural selection or at times due to chance mutation—traits that help them adapt more than their competitors, so as to sustain in a niche. A niche is a unique constellation of nurturing factors. A particular species is ideally suited to thrive in its niche. It tends to displace others. Between competing species, the one that is most ideally adapted to a niche survives in it in the long run. But the species do not consciously decide on how to survive, it happens as a natural process. Members of a species do not think or plan. They do not forecast, in advance, likely changes in the environment; nor do they make moves that make them more adaptable. They do not undertake any conscious analysis of the strengths and weaknesses of their rival; nor do they devise ways of coping with the same. They cannot think consciously. Yet, they compete through the process of natural adaptation. Competition between individual members of a species is more direct, more strongly rooted to a specific setting in time and space. Two dogs must fight for a bit of food, in a concrete time and space framework. They do not compete on the basis of evolving better, adaptive mechanisms to thrive in a niche: both share the same adaptive mechanism, appropriate to the stage of evolution they represent. Both attempt to thrive in the very same niche. In this case, the competition is likely to be somewhat more direct and violent. They may resort to sheer physical strength, and engage literally in 'dog-eat-dog' competition. Yet, even here there is a difference between the way humans often fight and the way dogs do. In a majority of these cases, the fight is deemed to be over when one of the contestants gives up his claim and accepts defeat. Seldom does one see a 'fight to finish'. This is, again, possibly due to the absence of 'foresight' in animals when it comes to the possibility of the phoenix rising from the ashes! In any case, the extent to which individual members of a species competing for survival have and use the faculty of logic, forecasting, anticipation, assessment and planning action, etc. is moot.

Competition among human beings or organisations (specifically business firms) is of a different nature. It is different in regard to both, the very objective for that competition and about the way that competition is played out in reality. Human beings are endowed with the instinct of accumulation; which, at times, appears as unfettered greed. (In an aside: an archetypal, aggressive capitalist—Ivan Boesky—told the graduating class of a leading business school in USA, 'by the way, there is nothing wrong with greed!' He, later, indulged in insider trading and went to cool his heels in jail.) Firms compete not merely because they need to survive, but because they wish to acquire good things such as money, wealth and power—well beyond what they need for survival and provisioning. (In another aside: the propensity for capital formation—the functional and constructive form of wealth accumulation—is to be found mainly among people who are relatively 'remote from nature'. Simple sons of the soil and children of nature, such as the tribal folk, lack this sense completely and live mainly in the 'subsistence mode'. Tribal folk live from year to year; enjoying the bounty of nature when it is bounteous; and scrounging for nourishment when nature frowns. They do not even engage in provisioning, let alone capital formation. This is really one of the single, most important hindering blocks faced by development professionals, who work towards improving the living standards of tribal people.)

Let us turn to ways of competing. Individual human beings think. They practice behaviours that seem to lead to desirable ends. They copy to learn such effective behaviours. They learn from observation and construct patterns, about events and about the behaviour of others. They project from these patterns. They have and can apply imagination. Hence, they think ahead. They can anticipate the likely course of events. They can assess the impact of likely events on their well-being. If necessary, they can take appropriate action to protect themselves and their well-being. They can anticipate likely behaviour of the rival, and devise ways of responding. They can introduce a decoy, a red herring. They may make a competitor believe that they will engage in one way of behaving and then, when he makes his move, change it all of a sudden. Thus, they may deceive, introduce diversionary tactics, and even practice what the Americans call 'the sting'. They can keep a whole repertoire of possible actions with them. They remain ready to put the right course into action, when needed. From naïve competitors, they become strategic competitors. Yet, it is useful to think whether some patterns of biology are not relevant to business situations as well. For instance, the competition between industrial units offering similar products may be compared with 'individual members of the same species', while industries may be compared with 'species'. The law that in the absence of differentiation, in the long run, only one among the species seeking to sustain from the same niche will survive; can be seen to have direct application. If niche can be translated into specific configuration of needs faced by a group of customers, then differentiation in terms of products and services is clearly the cardinal principle for industries and industrial units to survive. The 'dog-eat-dog' fight can be roughly translated into bloody price wars. The difference between business world and the world of animals is that there is often a fight to finish in the modern business world. Individual units and companies either die (fold up) or get 'eaten up' (acquired, etc.); while in the animal world, as we saw earlier, once a contestant accepts defeat he is then left to lick his wounds alone.

Mere competition for survival is one facet of the business situation that may need one to behave strategically and not naïvely. Conscious and deliberate effort to grow in size, reach and profitability is another reason why strategy may be required. While this may be so, it must be realised that all firms keep growing in some sense all the time. This may be called 'natural growth'. Growth in sales, net worth and profits is the most relevant for a business (economists would like to look at increase in value-added, as well as in employment); and this can come about through a variety of ways. Thus, growth may take many forms. Growth may come in an organisation because of two possibilities: either it puts up big projects, new factories, etc.—this is growth deliberately sought after; or, alternately, it may just grow in the course of time, without deliberate attempts. In the absence of deliberate action, propensities indicate the way things are likely to evolve in the course of nature. In a sense, this implies that such ways are natural, organic and perhaps, for that very reason, relatively safe and inexpensive. Some of this growth may occur due to demographic factors: the soap industry grows at the growth rate of population, combined with the growth rate of incomes. Natural growth comes about when a firm does more things in its own facilities; making marginal improvements or introduce changes here and there. This kind of growth indicated here is different from deliberate, well-planned projects that organisations undertake. Deliberate growth is more associated with strategy. Natural growth results from growth propensities. I address the question, 'how does natural growth come about?' I elaborate on growth propensities borrowing from Thompson.[1] Propensity means a natural tendency. There are three basic growth propensities, and they are the tendency towards balancing of components, the constant search for minimising coordination costs, and the play of discretion enjoyed by the powerful members of the dominant coalition of the organisation.

Balancing of Components

In common parlance, the word component refers to a small piece of fabricated metal in a machine. For instance, the carburetor is a component in a car. Here, I use the word in a similar, but slightly generalised sense. The word component may be used in the sense of a module, a group of people and their equipment in an organisation. Not all modules may be self-contained. For instance, the 'teaching faculty' is an important component in an institute of higher learning. They form a self-contained module; in the sense that they define their own work, standards of performance and can even become self-sustaining by selling their expertise outside. The secretarial pool in that institute is another module, if somewhat less self-contained. The 'transport section' including the vehicles and the drivers may form a module in another organisation, etc. In a manufacturing organisation, each department or section could be considered as a component. In a steel mill, the washed coal producing unit is a component, so are the blast furnace producing pig iron and the steel rolling mill.

---

[1] Thompson, JD; *Organizations in Action*, Prentice-Hall, Englewood Cliffs, NJ, 1967.

Ab initio, an organisation may be (and usually is) so designed that the capacities of individual components are adequate to meet the requirements of the organisation as predicted at that time; though it is very rare to have an organisation with exactly balanced components. This is because component capacities can seldom be equal. This is due to differences in 'natural units'. For instance, if an organisation decides to use mini-buses—each with a capacity to transport 16 people—then, the number of people to be transported from a certain department would only match by fluke; since the two components have different capacities. Similarly, a management institute may want a faculty to teach strategic management. Its need may just be for two courses for one section of students per year, but the capacity of the faculty member would hopefully be much larger! Thus, even *ab initio*, some components are likely to be used more than some others. There is greater slack in some components than in others. Slack is an unused resource for which one has paid. Under the norms of rationality, organisations like as little slack as possible. Hence, there is a tendency to deploy the slack component for 'some other productive work'. For example, the professor teaching strategic management could be asked to take on consultation work; to earn money for the organisation or to manage admissions.

As the organisation moves in time, the following things may happen:

- The demand for the 'main' products or services rises and the slack in all components start being used up. In fact, some components fall short of capacity; they become 'bottlenecks'. For example, hostel capacity may become a bottleneck for a growing institute. For a refrigerator company, its compressor-making unit may become a bottleneck.
- Demand for the 'some other productive use' of the components that had too much slack, *ab initio*, rises to such a level that it becomes almost as important as the 'main' product or service. For example, the demand for diesel generators made by a motorcycle company becomes so high that it becomes as important as the motorcycle line.

In either event, some components have to be added. As one knows, the developments in the field of virtually all technologies are fast increasing the minimum unit size. Previously, one could get a milk pasteuriser with the capacity for 500 litres an hour; now it may not be possible to get them with capacities below 1000 litres an hour. It is impossible to get an XT computer anymore. Not only do components come in lumpy capacities, these are increasing all the time. Thus, by the very nature of things, one may add much more capacity than is needed. This, then, creates a fresh slack. The tendency to try and maximise the use of available slack comes into force. The organisation tends to use it for some other productive purpose. As the growth occurs in that application, the slack disappears and bottlenecks appear—either in that or in some other component—and so on. The cycle continues. Do take note that growth occurs with the addition of every component, as well as with the use it is put to.

Constant Search to Minimise Coordination Costs

This is another driving force that enforces changes in the organisation agenda, including growth. There are, at least, two ways in which this drive works. For all the products and services that the organisation buys from outside to manufacture or ready its own products or services, the organisation has to incur transactions costs. Transactions costs cover search, bargaining and monitoring (including contract enforcement) costs. Every time a product or service is needed, possible suppliers are 'searched', bargaining on terms of service and price is carried on; and, then, there are costs associated with the supervision of the contract. To avoid this constant search, organisations maintain steady relations with one or a few suppliers. This is only the beginning of 'incorporation'. Diverse financial and organisational reasons may dictate that the concerned service or products be made within the organisation; the component for making it is acquired or incorporated. Having done this incorporation, there are the costs of managing the internal contingencies and coordinating from within. Should the organisation buy from the market or should it incorporate the relevant component into itself? These decisions are of the 'make or buy' type. The 'make or buy' or the 'incorporate or obtain from market' decision processes aim to balance the transactions costs and outflow of value to buy the product or service from outside; with the investment in incorporation and the routine coordination costs from within. Three factors influence this decision:

a) The intensity of dependence on the concerned item (higher the dependence, greater is the propensity for incorporation),
b) The volume in which it is required (high volumes justify own investment in manufacturing the component), and
c) The non-pecuniary values associated with it (would you like that the company chairman arrives in a hired taxi, or that he comes in his own limousine?).

As the interaction among these factors change the situation in time, the decision tends to swing from one side to another. *Each incorporation results in the growth of some kind.* It also adds another component to the 'balancing of component' cycle discussed above.

The type of dominant technology employed in the organisation tends to define the areas in which these forces of incorporation or buying from the market are felt. An organisation that deploys long-linked technology is likely to find greater problems of contingencies in acquiring inputs and in disposing off its inputs. Hence, it will have far greater occasions to add components at the input end or at the output end; resulting in backward or forward integration. Thus, long-linked technology firms tend to grow by vertical integration. Organisations employing mediating technologies (banks, insurance companies, transportation and courier companies, etc.) tend to become over-dependent on the small set of clients in rather well-defined and, perhaps, compact geographic areas. Economic fortunes of a compact geographic area, affect all the people at the same time. Uncertainties in market demand, etc., due to customer preferences or buying power, thus tend to be highly covariant—affecting the business of the firm very significantly. Hence companies deploying mediating technologies try to grow by reducing their relative dependence on them; either by expanding geographically, or by starting services to other groups of customers whose behaviour is not covariant with the extant ones. Thus, companies employing mediating technologies tend to grow by expanding the populations they serve. Finally, the companies employing intensive technologies find that the objects on which they work are the sources of the biggest contingencies. Management institutes discover that if students stay far apart from each other, then after-class group work becomes difficult. Management institutes then require students to stay in college hostels. Hospitals find that if patients do not follow the necessary diet and exercise regimen, and if their nursing is inadequate, their treatment is not effective. They, then, require them to be in-patients. Thus, such organisations grow by incorporating the objects worked on (students, patients, etc.).

The current buzzwords of rightsizing, by focusing on core competencies and outsourcing the rest, are directly relevant to this discussion. They just indicate that, perhaps, many organisations the world over were much towards the end of incorporating every possible thing into themselves. This is the hangover of the 'company township' culture in which the organisation wishes to have every possible thing, in-house. This was the culture of large integrated metal companies, or has been seen in most public sector units, etc.

The Third and the Most Interesting Propensity is Growth Due to Play of Discretion

It is allowed to, or enjoyed by, some key individuals. An expert food technologist was appointed the senior executive of NDDB, the dairy financing institution. Having a scientific bend of mind, he wished to experiment and develop techniques for mechanised manufacture of traditional Indian dairy products like *shrikhand*. His senior position gave him a lot of discretion in deploying his time and some money resources for this work. He used his discretion and ended up developing first-rate techniques for some products. These techniques then offered unique production technology, and became an important and highly rewarding source of growth. A famous scientist was appointed the non-executive chairman of Tata Chemicals, a large but somewhat conventional caustic soda unit. He used his discretion and made small investment in developing processes for isolation of some rare earths. (Rare earths are elements from the Periodic Table, atomic numbers between 58 and 67. Do you remember your chemistry?) While unrelated to the company's own product line, it offered some growth opportunities all the same. The son of Premji, a manufacturer of hydrogenated fats and soaps in Maharashtra, went abroad and studied about computers. On his return, he used his discretion as heir apparent to the company, to invest in the computer line. WIPRO is an IT giant today, and most youngsters do not even know about the company's oily origins!

I mention these three propensities because they tend to work in all organisations, all the time. And they work in a natural, intuitive manner. What is more, decisions involved in such propensities taking physical shape, may not appear as major decisions but as small incremental decisions. Only the cumulative impact of all these small decisions may be significant over time.

I had used the term strategic competition as an antithesis to naïve competition. The term, 'business strategy', certainly has some of this connotation. Yet, it needs to be understood properly. Let me refer to it now. Inferring directly from the above discussion on natural competition, the adoption of strategy implies an attempt at assessing:

- Likely shape of things to come,
- Possible behaviour of those who compete with the focal firm,
- Possible options for action,
- Their relative merits in terms of parameters of relevance,
- A conscious choice of one course, along with
- Preparedness for back up plan(s).

Such use of the word strategy was first made in military literature. The martial meaning of the word strategy is 'marshalling and deployment of forces for achieving a war objective'. The presence of competition is clearly at its sharpest in a military situation. Here, the need to forecast, guess the moves of the rival, assess various options, etc. acquires a very practical meaning. Strategy for a war is broader than the tactics for an encounter. Tactics refer to micro-manipulation of the resources in the short-term, to gain an advantage that has immediate relevance. Thus 'guerrilla techniques' or 'diversionary techniques' or 'setting up decoys' are all tactics, not strategies. Strategy is a superset of tactics.

Business theorists essentially borrow this concept of strategy. A 'rival army' is in the form of the sales and workforce of the numerous firms that make similar or substitute products; resources are the various techniques of persuading consumers, and ends are selling more of one's own products to earn more profits. Formally, *strategy is a statement of goals and means that is internally consistent and comprehensive to address all relevant external factors.* We look at each of the elements, in this statement, that defines strategy:

Goals

Corporate goals are typically in terms of statements of purposes, products, market-shares and profit or rate of interest targets. Corporate goals could, and these days often do, include statements regarding the environment, labour standards and impact on health and welfare of the community, etc. Sometimes the latter could be afterthoughts or add-ons, meant to acquire a favourable public image. (Of course, there is no cause for a general cynicism on this front.) A typical statement of goals could be:

'Our company aims to acquire a leadership position in cold rolled grain oriented (CRGO) steel laminates, transformers and armatures for the electric motor industry. We wish to achieve a market-share of not less than 30 per cent in the above market, in the next five years; and will aim for a net return on equity of not less than 50 per cent per year, from the third year onwards. While doing so, we shall ensure that our processes cause no damage to the environment and shall strive to further a sharing and nurturing culture in relation to the community.'

This statement makes it clear what the company will do: it will make and market CRGO steel, its laminates and make armatures of electric motors. No one can subsequently confuse the company's business. Efforts in the company in every sphere: research, process development, product development, application development, etc. will be targeted at this goal. There is possibly an error of over-specification, of narrowing down the efforts too much, of losing sight of opportunities that may arise and that may be cashed using essentially the same strengths as required for these products. There could also be a danger of the whole range of products becoming obsolete. As Levitt[2] argues, companies

---

[2] Levitt, T; *Marketing Myopia*, HBR, 1956.

ought to focus not on products but on the missions they serve. This goal also makes the target and the time horizon explicit: 30 per cent market-share in chosen product lines, in five years time. That is as specific as you can get. Finally, it decides the financial aim: 50 per cent return on equity; not return on investment, nor return on capital employed, but return on equity.

In general, specific goals

- Induce clarity
- Enable well-structured operations
- Direct and motivate action
- Enhance accountability, but
- May impose blinkers and could be myopic.

The last caution is necessary. Yet, it would be somewhat unusual for a business firm to state only its goals on sales, asset growth and profits—without stating what products and services will it offer. I have never come across a firm at least at the articulate level wanting 'to double the business and treble the net profit' from 'whichever items' it can procure and sale. Such an objective may become operative for essentially very new, raw or wholly flippant firms. (As I shall argue later, perhaps also for the most opportunistic firms.) While one may not be married to a business line for life, it is difficult to see how one can sell suit lengths this year and diesel engines the next, to achieve big growth. The degree of commitment to a product or service line perhaps differentiates between a pure mercantile capitalist and businessmen of the industrial era.

Means

A statement of goal comprises words that represent the direction in, and the distance to, which the company wishes to move. These words, by themselves, do not dictate action. A statement of means is all about action. Hence it is the operative part of the strategy, one may even call it the core strategy. An explicit statement of means may usually not be made, at least not prospectively, since it can easily allow for the preparation of formidable counter moves. This statement is thus to be reconstructed from the actions of a company. This does not mean that the company itself is unaware of the statement of means. The company is aware and has, usually, thought it out well. The statement of means with regard to a 'typical manufacturing and sales' company would involve sub-statements about:

- Which specific products in what sizes (colours, variants, etc.) would be introduced and in what phases;
- Which of the products and what proportion of them would be manufactured within the company and what would be outsourced;
- What manufacturing technology would be chosen, from whom it would be acquired, what would be the extent of its 'indigenisation' and over which time period;
- In what phases would the production facilities be built/ leased/acquired,
- How would the products be marketed and distributed (through own sales and logistic network, through own marketing but contracted logistics, through franchises, through commission agents, etc.),
- What is the key promotional theme, which particular segment is it addressed to, what is the chosen media-mix and the decided level of push-pull moves;
- What level of inventory is be maintained at different points in the supply chain, what would be the role of discounts and trade margins;
- What is the level of trade credits to be allowed, and so on.

It is quite conceivable that two organisations start with similar statements of goals but use very different means to attain the same. For example, a housing development company chooses for its goal: 'to become the largest single housing developer in Mumbai metropolitan area'. It would then have the choice of 'strategies'. It may invest money and acquire large tracts of land and contract out actual construction, it may decide to focus on architecture and construction as its strength and not invest in land but offer to develop plots of housing cooperative societies, it may decide to primarily focus on marketing and undertake land acquisition and building only when these cannot be 'outsourced', it may focus on building, on behalf of agencies like Small Industries Development Corporation Limited (SIDCO), Maharashtra Housing and Area

Development Authority (MHADA), etc. In terms of attracting customers, it may focus on a 'flexible payment plan with smooth facilitation of loans' or on 'no cost escalation come what may' or may announce that its commitment to the time of completion is inviolable. While some may focus on 'modern township' concepts, some others may focus on quality of construction and so on. Each of these is an observed strategy and each has its strong operational implication.

Internal Consistency

As seen above, the statement of means touches upon a large number of operational areas. These areas have inter-linkages and decisions on one invariably influence the space for decision-making on others.

- For example, if a company chooses the consistent, high quality of its products as the key element of its marketing strategy, then it may not have an option of outsourcing the products. It will have to install very systematic and rigorous quality assurance procedures, and will have to keep a very alert customer-service department. Absence of these elements, while attempting to use quality as a selling point, is an inconsistency.
- Let us look at another example. A company wishes to reach out to a very large number of customers, and also wishes to use trade credits to the customers as a competitive tool. Clearly it needs huge working capital to fund receivables. The company must do the following things or adopt similar tactics: enjoy similar large credit from suppliers on the input side, minimise inventories by adopting fast response logistics, and use consumer financiers upon terms of a negotiated agreement, as is done by the Indian auto industry now. Otherwise it would be an internally inconsistent strategy, and would choke the liquidity of the firm.
- A third example. A company wishes to engage in a business (such as IT, high fashion designs, etc.) that needs efforts of highly trained and bright people, who must develop and create their own products. Such people desire to have freedom. Application of the usual norms of discipline in

terms of work hours or dress codes or very tight and petty budget controls, etc. is completely inconsistent with the type of personnel who can make this business a success. One reason why the traditional *bania* business has not done well in IT in India is that few *banias* learned how critical this inconsistency could become. An institution of higher learning, in fact, lost a majority of its senior faculty resource within a matter of a few years after its imperious chairman unnecessarily made fixed office hours and muster roll mandatory.

In summary, inconsistency is eliminated by careful identification of requirements and implications of each of the decision being planned, resources required for it, its implications on other decisions, etc. Since many of these may be dynamic, the task of detecting and eliminating inconsistency is thus an ongoing task.

Comprehensively Addressing all Relevant External Factors

This is relatively easy to understand. Let us look at some examples. The manager of a famous dairy foods business insisted that he would make only such chocolates that met international standards. This means that the chocolate must melt when placed in the mouth, at around, say, 35 degrees centigrade. He insisted on this when cold storage chains were not common in Indian markets. The result was that his chocolates became a sticky, gooey mass in summers—children and parents alike developed an antipathy that is hard to remove even when cold chains have come into vogue. The firm never considered the ambient temperature and absence of cold chains while planning the marketing of chocolates. This is an example of failing to address a relevant environmental factor in the marketing strategy. The same could happen at the overall strategy level. An international marketer of children's garments began with a roar in Delhi, in the days of the myth of 'the 250 million strong Indian middle class'—only to shut down to lick its wounds and reformulate its strategy, a few months later. The relevant reality was that few buyers were willing to pay Rs 750 for a T-shirt for their three year old.

To make the strategy work, the firm needs to understand the key environmental factors to do with inputs as well as outputs; get a hold on factors driving them, and plan by thinking carefully how its actions would affect and be influenced by these factors. An Indian multinational contemplated entry into frozen vegetables. It discovered that the production of the vegetables it needed was so dispersed, and the markets so shallow and thin, that its entry into the raw vegetable markets to feed its proposed plant would double the prices. This would make the production economics go topsy-turvy. The company had to shelve the plan. This is one example of how careful understanding and analysis of the market forces, can help you appreciate the impact of your actions on the key factors that define viability. In fact, the whole countryside is teeming with sick, small industry units installed by people who did not think carefully about the business environment; and simply jumped into bankruptcy. With sensitivity analysis and scenario building becoming simpler, it is a criminal folly not to undertake fairly critical ex-ante analysis before launching the strategy. After the launch of the strategy, it is important to keep monitoring the relevant external factors to see whether they behave in the manner initially thought out, and, if not, then how would they affect the firm; and what could be done to avoid their negative consequences.

To summarize, then:

- Strategy of a firm is the statement of goals and means that is internally consistent and comprehensively addresses all relevant external factors;
- The statement of goals needs to be quite clear, precise and both, inspiring as well as achievable;
- Statement of means need not be made public but, internally, it must be sufficiently clear about the exact combination of decisions on products, production and distribution logistics, pricing, promotion etc.; so as to speed up implementation;
- Internal consistency refers to the interactive nature of these decision areas, and its absence is usually disastrous; and
- Comprehensive treatment of external factors is necessary ex-ante, along with continuous monitoring once started, to adjust internal actions to ensure consistency.

Components of Strategy

Conventional literature[3] on strategy identifies four components of strategy: *product-market posture, growth vector, competitive edge* and *synergy*. The same is supplemented by a more recent addition that these components are woven together, consistent with the *values* of the management. We look at these five aspects of strategy. Let us begin with values.

Values in Management

The word value is used by economists in the sense of worth such as in 'realisable value', 'use value' etc. The former is the amount of cash one would get, if a particular asset was sold in the market. Use value is the value derived due to use of the object, etc. We wish to use the word value in an ethical sense. We regard a 'value' as a firmly cherished state of the world or society, held dear by the person having such a value. Some examples:

- 'Sanctity of free markets and perfect competition' is the dominant value of the capitalist world.
- 'Secularism' is a value held dearly by India.
- I hold the value of professional integrity as being supreme.
- Non-violence, truth, simple living and universal brotherhood are well-known Gandhian values.
- Liberty, equality and fraternity were the values advocated by the French revolutionaries.

A value is beyond debate, argument and assessment. One does not evaluate whether it is worth having that value. Yet, one may desire to assess other things on the criteria derived from the values one holds dear.

People comprising the top management of a firm have their values; and would usually stick along together in a team, only when they share these values. A firm's management may be staunchly nationalistic, and would make no compromise on that matter even when the economy is going global. Such a firm may

---

[3] Igor, Ansoff H; *Corporate Strategy*, McGraw Hill, New York, 1965.

prefer to go down fighting, rather than sell off to an MNC. The management of a firm may strongly believe in putting its people first and, hence, would renounce business decisions that require large-scale retrenchments. Self-respecting men of honour run some firms and these firms do not behave in the fly-by-night style of those 700 firms that came out with public issues in 1992–94, but were not even traceable in 2001. People, who believe that their objective in life is to make money and not be too finicky about its smell or colour, may run other firms. These firms may be seen adopting whichever means to make quick bucks. RC Sekhar[4] discusses the role of values in management, in detail.

How do values influence decisions? Some concrete examples:

a) A car company discovers that some 50 pieces out of the factory have a problem that can cause accidents. What should it do?

- Wait for the defect to surface over time, and claim that it was not a manufacturing defect. After all, Indian courts are said to take decades to settle a case and, hence, the company would have to pay nothing, really.
- Trace the buyers and write to them, asking them to bring the pieces back for necessary retrofitting.
- Issue expensive advertisements in national newspapers, asking people to bring back the cars for repairs.

All the three behaviours are observed.

b) A less extreme example. Producers of chocolates and biscuits know that, under the most commonly prevalent movement and stocking systems in Indian trade and retail chain, there is a good chance of a chocolate or a biscuit pack becoming bad in, say, four months' time. What should they do?

- Initiate a system wherein they call back all unsold the stock, at the end of four months.
- On their own volition, print 'best before' messages along with the possible causes of the product getting affected.

---

[4] Sekhar, RC; *Ethics in Management*, Response Books, New Delhi, 1997.

- Issue public interest notices occasionally, educating consumers about the shelf life of these products.
- Ensure that there is free replacement of all bad pieces returned by consumers? (There is a catch here: consumers are unlikely to go to a retailer to replace a five rupee pack; and not all retailers are likely to be so courteous as to promptly replace bad goods.)
- Sell outdated stock at a discount, to poor children.
- When an occasional angry consumer throws a rotten pack in your managers' face and threatens to go to press, bribe him with expensive gift packs.

I have had the last experience with two multinational chocolate brands, in the past five years.

c) A third example, from consumer finance. You are a company with an international reputation. You run a sister concern that has made a big name in software development. You make some arbitrary charges to many a borrower in consumer loan accounts, as well as in credit card accounts. What you do when such a borrower writes a stinker is maintain complete silence till he threatens legal action, or bad publicity. Then, you write to him that 'the wrong charge was made due to a computer error' and do not even say sorry. Then, despite your billion-dollar tag, you are just a cheap, two-penny, shifty-eyed trader who cannot be trusted as far as one can throw a credit card. Or, is making money when the consumer is not looking, your value?

To return to strategy, whether explicitly or implicitly, the values held dear by the management inevitably influence the choice they make in their decision-making. They leave a strong mark on the way things are done. Closely allied with values, but of less austerity is the issue of personal style. A chief executive's behaviour reflects both, his values and his style. Both affect others in the firm and, hence, the range of choices that are considered by the others as prima facie acceptable. Style refers to orientation in relating to others: some people are aggressive, autocratic and adamant. Recall the famous statement attributed to Henry Ford, 'I shall make any car as long as it is Model T, and I shall paint it any colour as long as it is black.' The CEO of a famous American company, known for his insistence on honesty, is said to have squashed an ad jingle, 'day after day, in every home, people are saying there is nothing like (his soft drink)'. He did so because he said that he knew people do not say this! Style definitely influences the nature of choices people make. In Chapter six of my book *How Not to Ruin Your Small Industry*,[5] I have suggested three styles of entrepreneurs: the lion style, the lizard style and the style of the fox. The lion is a dare devil, ambitious, bold and, perhaps, a risk lover who plays for big stake. The lizard is the man who believes in making money unobtrusively, without making too much fuss about company pride or image, etc. The fox avoids fights if he can negotiate, but does not lose sight of his objective; and could turn into a lion when he gains strength.

In summary, both, values and strategy, influence the pattern of decisions; and since they do, it is best to consider them explicitly rather than allow their influence to seep in surreptitiously.

Product-Market Posture

Product-market posture defines the business of the firm, and is characterised by *what products/services* the firm offers *to which markets*, and for *which end uses*. This is then generalised to ask, 'what mission does the firm serve?' The conventional way of asking this question is 'what business is the firm in?'
Some examples:

- An IT training firm like NIIT may be (and this is only my conjecture, not NIIT's official statement) in the business of *preparing Indian students and executives for careers in information technology*. The 'product' is understood as the range of software, possibly hardware and certainly applications courses. The 'market' comprises young undergraduates, graduates and working persons who seek to enter the field of IT. The end use of the courses is entry into a professional career, not application in one's own office or home. Contrast this with another, smaller firm called Jetking, which focuses mainly on hardware courses and prepares young graduates

---

[5] Phansalkar, SJ; *How Not to Ruin Your Small Industry*, Response Books, New Delhi, 1996.

for careers in the field of hardware: computer maintenance, networking, etc. Another firm could, perhaps, focus only on training in web design; some could focus only on multimedia applications, etc. We do see examples of such firms. NIIT appears to have a wider range of courses.

- A firm called Kirloskar Cummins (now Cummins India) decided that its business was production of a range of diesel engines. These engines could then be applied in various ways: in generator sets, marine applications, etc. The firm, perhaps, designed and developed engines that were ideal for such applications. The product was diesel engines, the market comprised those who needed to use diesel engines, and the applications or end uses were diverse.

- The Bohra suppliers to the plantation companies of yester-years—all, focused on clients rather than on products. Their clients were located in estates quite removed from markets, and the supplier would be their nodal point to procure food stuff, fertilisers, medicines, general items and, sometimes, services like railway tickets, taxis and even emergency access to medical professionals. Their 'product' was facilitating the clients in acquiring whatever they desired. The market was clearly defined as the estates. End uses were clearly defined by the clients.

It is important to recognise that product-market posture can become stable only if there is a degree of 'domain consensus' on it. This means that the buyers of these products, other sellers of these services and, where relevant, the regulators and other resource providers —all, must agree that it is right and proper that the focal firm offers these products and services. Over time in its exchanges with the market, the firm's product-market posture gets stabilised through this domain consensus. The firm gets 'pigeon-holed'. The firm's business actions, relating to its own product-market, are expected and do not even get noticed. However, when it does anything pertaining to other products or markets, the business community takes notice. For instance, as long as Reliance Infocomm does things on the lines of telecom, broadband, Internet, etc.—no one will notice specifically. Yet, if it did something to do with, say, building railway bridges—people will sit up and look at it with interest! Thus, basically, product-market posture through domain consensus gives the firm a personality, a public image and that, in turn, sets in expectations about the firm's subsequent actions. Its actions in other areas are seen as less than completely serious. For instance, a group of small industrialists of Nagpur, all engaged in metals or such other engineering lines, got together and set up a strawberry farm near Nagpur. When they held a press conference at the end of the season, it was thought to be a big joke, a kind of pastime for rich men's amusement, not as a serious business activity. When the daughter-in-law of a famous tractor-maker in north India set up a chain of super stores in and around Delhi, people thought it to be quite interesting, but did not regard it as a serious business move of the group.

What business one is in, also defines what one will not do. The advantages of defining product-market posture are that it *permits focus*, facilitates *development of expertise*, generates advantages of *learning curve* and opens up possibilities of *scaling up in terms of volumes as well as regions served, both for the same products*. On the other hand, this may become *restrictive*; may, at times, *entail loss of promising opportunities*, and may become highly counter productive either when the market shrinks due to demographic reasons or when substitute products enter the picture. That is why Levitt had recommended that firms must focus on the missions— the end uses that their products serve—and not just the products in their specific detail.

The Indian scene is interesting in this regard. The history of business reveals that business firms arose from two classes: traders and moneylenders. Hence, the term 'mercantile capitalism' is used. The traders were and, to an extent even now, are not committed to a specific product in the sense of developing expertise in its manufacture or applications. They may focus a little on applications and servicing, since these are supplementary to the trade. People hesitate to buy a complex device unless they feel that the seller will stay with them while they learn how to use it and how to maintain it, so the traders do the needful. Traders believe in buying cheap and selling at the best price they can get. Moneylenders are primarily interested in the interest they get on the loans they give. The world over, this background of business has implied the rise of the trading houses. Sometimes they may become like conglomerates—this word refers to a business organisation that may offer a wide variety of products unrelated *entre-se* in terms of raw materials or manufacturing technology. The eastern businesses, including the so-called 'large business houses' of India, were mostly trade-houses turning into conglomerates. The whole concept of focused mission emerged when the manufacturing activity emerged from the artisans' yards and the guilds became possible after mass manufacturing. The logic of technology spurring expansion in forward or backward direction, etc. started and, by now, has more or less become dominant business theology. Yet, even in twenty-first century India, the firms retain essentially the mercantile capitalist flavour at the lower end of business. It is not uncommon to see a business house simultaneously engaged in diverse and unrelated activities. A business group with a size of a few hundred crores, headed by Banwarilal Purohit for instance, runs a mini-cement plant, publishes newspapers, runs educational institutions, and makes and sells hydrogenated oils. In fact, practically the whole class of *marwari* and *bania* business houses (e.g., the Birlas, Modis, Goenkas, Bangurs, etc.) has been run in this fashion. The concept of 'management agency' that was in vogue in the country, further buttressed this trend. Even the House of Tatas was in this class. It is only with the post 1950 'first generation entrepreneurs' that the concept of a sharply defined mission has taken some, though not firm, root. Till the Eighties, curbs on growth under the Monopolistic and Restrictive Trade Practices (MRTP), Act and all manners of non-productive incentives (100 per cent export house benefits, backward area benefits, rents of securing licenses, etc.) weakened the development of a focused business entity. It is true, though amazing, that the consumer product company like Hindustan Lever had once acquired a license to manufacture cement; had actually entered the fertilizers business, and had toyed with the export of bicycles and handicrafts. None of these had anything to do with their 'core business'. Even a post-Seventies firm like Dr Reddy's Laboratories (DRL) had got into all kinds of business; from lease finance to computer peripherals, and even halogen lamps! However, the current environment seems to put a premium on focus. One expects that the future growth would come to those who define and strengthen their sharply defined missions in India.

In summary, the way businesses will look at their mission is quite contingent on the economic environment and cultural ethos.

Growth Vector

Growth Vector[6] defines how a firm plans to grow in terms of activity levels: in case of typical business firms, sales and profits. Business firms usually have growth ambitions. Seldom do business firms explicitly decide not to grow. Absence of growth is stagnation. Owners of closely held companies, themselves, have growth ambitions. Shareholders of large corporations seek appreciation of their investments and, hence, nudge their management to seek to grow. Even when neither is explicit, growth is deemed necessary for the firm to maintain itself. When the staff sees their firm stagnating, they infer that they have no opportunities for personal growth. Their motivation levels drop. They seek greener pastures. Absence of growth deprives the firm of market standing, and the cash much needed to replace or upgrade assets. Soon an aggressive competitor takes over and, since business competition is more brutal than natural competition, the firm faces extinction. Thus growth is a business imperative. I have argued that even for small and medium enterprises in India, run by contented owners who seek self-fulfillment in walks of life other than business growth, growth is a categorical imperative. Grow or go, that is the basic message.

Growth can come in several ways. The firm may sell more of the same products to the same consumers, by inducing them to buy more of its products in preference to those of the competitors. The firm may expand the customer base by expanding regionally or nationally. The firm may introduce allied products for the same customers. Or, the firm could introduce new products for a whole new market. This is captured in Figure 3.1.

The words old and new are used relative to existing markets or products. Introduction of a whole range of new products for new markets is called *diversification*. For example, Telco manufactured a range of commercial vehicles for goods or passenger transport. Their market comprised fleet owners, and public or private bus operators. When Telco (now Tata Motors) introduced the multi-utility vehicle *Sumo*, it was a diversification since the product was new and the market was also new. *Indica* made for further diversification. As this example shows, diversification may

---

[6] This discussion borrows from Igor, Ansoff H; op. cit.

Figure 3.1: Products vis-à-vis the market

Products

		New	Old
Markets	New	Diversification	Repositioning or Geographic Expansion
	OLD	Line Widening	Penetration

be sufficiently rewarding, so as to make the company relegate the original business to a less important position.

Usually a firm growing by catering to the existing set of customers, does so either by increasing its market-share or by converting non-users into user groups (both, cases of penetration) or by introducing new products that meet other needs of the customers. When new products are thus introduced, they are usually related to existing products in some fundamental way determined by consumer/buyer behaviour. This is called product-line widening. Hindustan Lever grows by introducing new types of personal products or detergents to its basic customer base comprising the middle and higher class of urban consumers. In the Seventies they introduced *Liril* soap, *Close Up* toothpaste and the *Wheel* as well as *Vim* range in the Eighties, and introduced *Surf Excel* detergents in the Nineties. The product class was the same. The product line was, thus, made wider. Telco widened its product line by introducing medium and light commercial vehicles for lighter loads and smaller distances. When Hindustan Lever grows by making more rural buyers take to using soap, it amounts to penetration. Pepsi, in India, has major growth plans by increasing the per capita, per year consumption from some nine bottles to 12, 15 or 30 bottles—by increased penetration, that is. When the number of consumers is unlikely to grow much, the company may seek to grow by making consumers buy its products in preference to that of the competitors. This happens when the markets are growing 'only at demographic rates'. Sun Pharmaceuticals was strong in the eastern region in the early Eighties. Initially, the company grew by expanding sales of its products (medicines like tranquillisers, used in psychotropic therapy) in other regions. This was growth by *geographic expansion*. Eicher is attempting the same, by trying to sell its tractors in central and south India. When Pidilite introduced the same adhesive in ultra small packages, for use by children in making paper craft; this was a case of product repositioning. The company making M-Seal did similar repositioning. The path for growth or the growth vector chosen by firms depends on two basic factors: their *goals* and the *opportunity as well as the management's perception of relative rewards*, for possible new activities. For example, BASIX, a new generation rural, financial institution is committed—by its corporate goals— to offering a range of financial products like loans, savings, insurance and risk mitigation products such as futures. While, so far, its main line has been that of offering a range of loan products to small farmers; it seeks to widen this range to include other products, over a period of time. This is a goal driven growth vector. The second factor is opportunity and the perception of relative rewards. In the late Nineties, Hindustan Lever perhaps thought that the relative rewards in product lines such as *atta* and ice cream were superior to those in demographically growing markets for personal products and soaps. The growth vector must make the firm move into products and markets that are compatible with its original product-market posture. Normally, a Hindustan Lever would not consider setting up a chit fund company or a collective investment scheme of teak plantation. A Telco is quite unlikely to start marketing furniture, steel safes or even tractors. Now we see the era of focused firms, not of mercantile capitalists. Cases of wholly unrelated diversification (that is when products, markets as well as technology, raw materials and marketing channels are all different) are usually rare now.

Competitive Edge

This refers to the basic reason why the firm is, or is hoped to be, able to outperform its competitors. The competitive edge could come in the form of superior product features (e.g., laser printers vs. inkjet printers, or inkjet vs. dot matrix printers for typical office use), low cost positions (the fear of the edge of Chinese products, as in 2001), distribution muscle (Hindustan Lever can push its *atta* through thousands of retail points, Dinshaw's *Param Atta* has fewer retail outlets), proven track record of high quality of products, legal protection as in intellectual property rights, etc. Some of these features could be real, some make-believe. The point is, the firm must decide what specific feature about its business will become, or will be made, its competitive edge; and take necessary action to make it so.

Synergy

Alternately summed up in the magical formula '2+2 = 5', synergy refers to that attribute of the company's business that can be deployed between two product lines to the advantage of both. The advantage comes in the form of cost reduction; achieved through sharing of facilities, R&D, raw materials, distribution channels, etc.

The word synergy is irrelevant if the firm makes only one product or offers only one service. Again, the advantage is vis-à-vis the competitor who does not have that particular attribute. For instance, the technology of making compact, high performance IC engines is Honda company's synergy across a range of products: motorcycles, diesel generator sets, gardening equipments, etc. Competitors engaged in each of these individual product lines would not possess this synergy, and would have a disadvantage while competing with Honda. In the Indian context, massive distribution muscle is the synergy used by Hindustan Lever, between detergents and *atta*. Press barons seek to use the access to high speed printing facilities, to bring about a synergy between newspapers and other periodicals.

The body of the management discipline that deals with these issues is called strategic management. This body believes that most businesses have a strategy. This strategy may not be explicit and articulated, but it exists 'at the back of the mind'. Much analysis and pontification is done—alas, almost always retrospectively about the soundness of the strategy! Analysts try to piece together the sequence of actions of the business organisation in question and then 'reconstruct' the strategy. Yet, to say that a business existed and flourished for a long time without any—even implicit—strategy at its base, would be considered unusual, if not a very heretical statement. There are two other collateral issues that may interest some of the readers. First is the question of the relevance of strategy to non-profit organisations. I ignore this. And the second is the question of the assessment of strategy. This is covered in Annex I to this chapter.

Competitive Strategy

I now return to the need for a competitive strategy, a subject dealt with at length, and most competently, by Porter.[7]

One must understand the nature of competition faced by a firm, before one can plan its competitive strategy. The firm faces current competition from other firms making and offering the same product and service, or some other product or service that serves the same mission. Competition among firms making similar products for serving the same mission is called 'industry competition.' The competition among all units making ceiling fans is, thus, industry competition. But the indirect competition between air coolers and the technology to make building walls with partly hollow bricks and ceilings covered with brick bat *goba* is not an industry competition; but is a more general competition. Both serve the same mission of keeping the room temperature within a comfortable limit.

Irrespective of whether customer demand is met by a similar product of the competitor, or by substitute products or services, the fact remains that the focal firm experiences reduced demand. Thus, it is important to look not only at current industry competition but also the general competition to a firm. We first look at the general competitive picture.

The structure of general competition is made up of five factors. The most immediate of these is, of course, *industry competition*. We discuss this at length, later in this book.

1. Backward Integration by Buyers

There is a possibility that customers, themselves, take up the manufacture or preparation of the firm's product. *Thus, the buyers threaten to enter the industry and compete by making the product.* As

---

[7] Porter, from among his many books, *Competitive Strategy* (the discussion follows his exposition), Free Press, New York, 1980.

long as they do so only to the extent that they meet their own demand, the firm has lost only one customer. But when the buyer discovers that it can make enough of the product to sell it to others, then the competition becomes real. Here is an example, at home. As a working bachelor, you regularly eat in a restaurant. Then one day, you hire a cook and start making food at home. So far, the restaurant owner has lost only one customer, and he is not too worried. But then, a dozen of your colleagues discover that you really have a flair for preparing excellent meals and that your cook is a direct disciple of Sanjeev Kapoor. So all of you pool in your resources and start cooking and eating meals together, regularly. Thus, really bringing down the demand of the restaurant.

Another example, from the industry: the firm GKW made CRGO steel for laminates required in transformers. Jyoti was one of the customers. Jyoti also made high HP motors and similar equipment that needed CRGO steel. Jyoti decides to make its own CRGO steel and GKW loses just one customer. But later, when Jyoti starts making enough CRGO steel to supply to the pump industry in Gujarat, then the competition becomes serious.

The buyer will decide to buy your product from you or he will make it himself, depending on a whole set of factors: technology, minimum economic lot of production vis-à-vis his demand, competency in handling the manufacture, sourcing of raw material, etc. This follows the logic of comparison of transactions cost with incorporation costs, which we discussed in an earlier note. Having started making it himself, the buyer may initially want to sell to others only from the slack capacity. Jyoti needs 500 MT of CRGO steel but has a capacity for 1000 MT, so it tries to sell 500 MT so that its unit cost comes down. But later, what can happen is that the buyer may discover that he has 'boot-strapped' and developed an operational technology that gives him a competitive advantage over you; and that the fact he consumes a part of the product only gives him greater sense of security. So he starts marketing the product extensively.

2. Forward Integration by Suppliers

The mirror image of this phenomenon is that the suppliers of the crucial materials or components may start making the products of the firm by forward integration. *Thus, suppliers threaten to enter by making the product that the firm makes.* For example, let us suppose that Tata Iron and Steel Company Limited (TISCO) makes and supplies steel to Wheel and Axle Plant that makes these parts for the Railway. The plant would then forge the steel into wheels, etc. TISCO could set up forging facilities and make wheels and axles, and supply them to the same, ultimate buyer. Thus, the Wheel and Axle Plant faces a lurking threat from TISCO—*their* supplier entering *their* business. In the case of Jyoti and GKW, the latter could start making transformers and compete with Jyoti.

3. Substitute Products

There always is an active possibility *of substitutes serving the same mission coming into the market.* For a while, bright and shining silver utensils were replaced with aluminum ones which carried so much prestige in its early days that even the British Empress owned an aluminum dinner set. For that limited time, both the metals served the same mission of offering material to make 'snob-value' dinnerware. In India, the transportation of goods is experiencing a slow shift from railways to roadways. While both these services have no technical commonalities, they serve the same mission of transportation and, hence, act as a substitute for each other. Funnily enough, public sector buses act as an indirect substitute for two-wheelers for office goers. In mid-size cities when buses become unreliable, take too long or when she learns that she may be harassed in a crowded bus, many a working, middle-class woman chooses to buy a two-wheeler. Both, the bus and the two-wheeler, serve the same mission of urban transport to commuting office-goers. Bill Gates has argued that hotel industry will experience a severe downturn when teleconferencing via the net becomes cheap and commonplace—to the extent that these two will serve the same mission of facilitating face-to-face business conferencing. Similarly there is much talk since March 2001, about how Wireless in Local Loop (WiLL) telephony will substitute mobile phones for a high share of the latter's total market.

4. Lateral Entry

Finally, some entrepreneur currently not in the industry itself, nor in its supplier or buyer industries, may decide to enter the business to make and sell the product if he finds it to be an attractive proposition. This is the *threat of a lateral entry*. New actors continue to enter the burgeoning IT training business. At the level of an individual, Hindi film actresses must fear the threat of such a lateral entry all the time, as several *debutantes* become instant hits; leaving the incumbents with their bookings cancelled and their businesses dwindling. In rural areas, the established, informal moneylenders and traders managed to survive the entry of nationalised banks, cooperative banks and such institutions—but are now being hit badly as self-help groups, supported by dynamic micro-finance institutions, become an increasingly dominant source of credit to the poor.

5. Industry Competition

The intensity of competition in an industry is really a function of three things—how lucrative and growing the market for its products is, how easy it is to enter the industry and how easy it is to exit it. Ease of entry is determined by the presence, or otherwise, of *entry barriers*. These are things that make it difficult for a new firm to enter the business. For example, it is far more complex and difficult to enter the business of industrial explosives than to foray into readymade garments. To make industrial explosives, one needs access to a complex technology, a series of approvals, etc. One extremely expensive requirement is that of space, to ensure that production process and stores are sufficiently removed from residential areas. Another is the staying power to block capital for the few years that it takes for these explosives to be cleared for sale. Readymade garment making, on the other hand, needs a low level investment in sewing machines, organising a lot of labour for stitching, etc.; and enough working capital to last through the working capital pipeline. The result is evident in that each year sees the launch of dozens of new brands of readymade garments; while there are only a few new entrants in the line of industrial explosives.

Ease of exit is a mirror image of the entry barrier problem. These are called *exit barriers*. These may be labour law hurdles, the Indian industry keeps bemoaning about. Closing an industrial unit, in India, is as tough as starting one. There may be highly ´ dedicated facilities that simply have no possible market value and, hence, liquidation losses are immense. Often, the biggest exit barriers could be the inability of the owners of the firm to accept defeat and start doing something else.

The more lucrative and growing an industry, less intense may be the competition in it—as compared to the competition in a stagnant and less profitable industry. If the pie is growing very fast, you do not really mind the share of your neighbour's slice. If the pie shrinks, you carefully watch for shares and jealously protect yours. If one compares the degree of intensity in the three segments of the computer and IT business, one may find that the hardware maintenance sector grows much slower and has higher competition; followed by the hardware sales line. Finally, the software training line which experiences the most rapid growth has the least intense competition.

We may now revert to our theme of competitive strategy. The extent to which a company depends on a particular product line and the degree of its involvement, as indicated by its market-share in that line, together influence the competitive strategy of the firm, for that product line. I may totally depend on consultancy for my livelihood, but I am perhaps a very small player for big-time consulting firms to worry about me. Conversely, I may not even think of them when planning my competitive strategy. In general, firms dependent on particular lines and having big shares in the business in that line (e.g., Ashok Leyland in trucks, ITC in tractors, ACC in cement, etc.) have to worry about competitive strategy. It may be noted that such firms also face huge exit barriers in that line; for if they exit, they may not exist at all!

Competitive strategy is often formulated at two levels. In the first place, there may be strategic moves to *discourage, forestall, or obviate* entry of new players in the industry. This way the chosen few firms in the industry continue to share the market among themselves. In regulated economies, this is the easiest thing to do. Till the licensing regime was in force, new entries could be forestalled in virtually every line by 'cornering licenses'. This was done through applications for so much capacity in devious ways, so that all the planned capacity was allotted to a coterie and newcomers could just not get permission to start business. This is precisely what happened in India in the Sixties, and the GoI appointed the Dutt Committee of Inquiry to look into the charges of licenses being cornered. Regulations can also come in the form of quantitative regulations or tariff rates on imports, and can be used to keep outsiders at bay. Look, for instance, at how the Indian auto industry screamed in almost unison, against the entry of second-hand cars and managed to win the day by hiking customs duty to 185 per cent in the 2001 Budget. That is their way of making the entry of second-hand car sellers, in Indian auto industry, difficult. They used the duty structure for this. Indian press barons are whipp·ng up nationalistic sentiments to forestall entry of foreign papers in the country. Many a country belonging to the European Union and the 'first world' routinely misuse the bogey of chemical or biotic contamination or such other 'non-tariff, non QR' trade barriers to protect their own industry. For instance, after decades of purchasing textiles from India, the Germans suddenly found that azo dyes could cause itching to their dogs or mice or whatever—and banned the imports of readymade garments from India! One uses a route called 'lobbying', to achieve all this. This is often used and mostly behind the door; by the whole industry rather than one firm, and is the cause of several scams and political corruption. For instance, during 1994–98, it is said that the entry of the SIA-Tata combine in the domestic aviation was forestalled by a domestic airline through sheer lobbying. The combine finally got sick of it all, and gave up the plan. Other ways of forestalling or obviate entry could be to:

- Tie up all sources of critical inputs or the whole distribution channel,
- Raise the scale of investment to a level where few can afford the risk, and
- Introduce such switching costs that customers would find very difficult to get over, etc.

A final, interesting, but perhaps masochistic tool is what is called 'entry deterring price'. In this method, one reduces the price of the product around the time the competitor is preparing to launch his product, and to such a level that the competitor finds it impossible to sustain himself. The latter recognises that he is in for a big bloody fight if he enters, and hence postpones or abandons his plans. As a new entrant, he must incur huge set up cost, promotion and trade inventory costs and so on; and, if the price that he gets is reduced to close to or even below the variable cost, he simply cannot cope for too long. This is a popular tool for harassing small competitors but is very expensive if tried against industrial giants, since they may have deeper pockets.

Yet, in most countries, consumer pressures articulated through democratic structures and economic realities, work against permanently eliminating new entry. So, strategic thinking has to proceed about how to compete. Porter has identified three generic strategies for a competitive posture. These are cost leadership, differentiation and focus.

Cost Leadership

Cost—and not price leadership—is the strategy in which the firm has cost advantages over all the existing and, perhaps, many of the potential competitors. The firm could enjoy low cost because it has access and ownership of the best raw materials (such as the mining rights over the best ore deposits), is optimally located, has acquired specific cost advantages due to experience (learning) curve because of its long-standing presence, has set up huge facilities that permit great economies of scale, enjoys significant synergy in manufacturing across related products, can exploit really cheap labour, and so on. The point is that this cost leadership permits the firm to compete, by offering superior price-quality product profile to customers. It also allows the firm to earn additional margins that can be reinvested to further strengthen its cost leadership. On the flip side, this strategy may not always be possible as it is difficult for newcomers; and exclusive reliance on cost leadership may induce complacence about product features and quality. Finally, the arrival of substitute products may also render cost leadership irrelevant.

Differentiation

Differentiation, as a generic competitive strategy involves careful assessment of the current profile of customer needs and available solutions and, through both product development and positioning, taking up a position that is recognised by the whole industry as being unique and different from any other competitor. This position is assumed by the firm and is effective only if the task environment accepts and legitimises it. Differentiation is thus a combination of product positioning, niche marketing, building special and uncommon features into the product and creating an image of exclusivity. This can reduce effective market reach as many potential customers may self-select themselves out of the market.

Both cost leadership and differentiation are strategies that are taken by the firm across all range of customers and, in fact, in the entire industry as such.

Focus

As the term suggests, the firm may evolve a strategy of focusing on a customer class or geographic region or a specific application of the product. An eveninger like *MidDay* focuses on the angli-cized, commuter populace in Mumbai. A company named Eureka Forbes focuses on the readership of modern, higher-middle class, urban consumers and sells directly to them. Some ready-to-eat foods may be available only in the National Capital Region (NCR) on which their sellers focus. Such focus allows them to concentrate attention on a relatively homogeneous, compact territory and manage it efficiently. It need not necessarily reduce the market demand one can reach out to. Let us take the last case. There are over 4000 retailers of the daily-needs sort in the NCR; and they cater to over 13 million of the consumers with, perhaps, much higher disposable incomes than consumers elsewhere. This market is large enough for a small company and is prudent to focus on. For instance, a single bottle of jam or pickle of the company sold by each retailer, every day, would amount to a respectable sale of 1.4 million bottles, valued perhaps at a few crores! The disadvantage with focus strategy is that the rest of the market assumes that the company products are not meant for them. The company may become preoccupied with the chosen customer group, and may not notice lucrative opportunities elsewhere. This way the company strengths may become cripplingly over-specific.

These were generic strategies. At a particular level, competitive strategy of a company could be based on one of several specific strengths or actions. Some of the more noteworthy strengths, their positive points and associated risks are mentioned in the table below. The last column mentions the requisites for it to be an effective competitive tool.

Devoid of any of the earlier six competitive tools mentioned in Table 3.1, most small and medium firms in India adopt the last two tools—namely, price-cutting and long credit periods. Both strategies are decidedly myopic and self-defeating. Price-cutting may win a sale, but it also makes two statements: one about the quality of the product and the other about your intention of overcharging if a customer does not bargain. Neither creates a respectable image for the firm. Long credit periods may, sometimes, be forced upon the seller but, when used as a competitive strategy, it will surely impair liquidity. Also, capacity utilisation will be reduced since the total working capital available is bound to be limited.

Annex I: Assessment of Strategy

So far, I have discussed several aspects of the concept of business strategy: its need, the formal construction of the concepts, its components, its relevance to non-competitive businesses and its specific relevance and form for competing. I now turn to assessment of strategy. To begin with, let me record a view that corporate strategy exists mainly in retrospect. This view holds that, while management of corporate organisations do have a broad road map about the way their company would do business in future, seldom do they have a plan that is fully worked out. Business is too complex and dynamic for that. In the first place, corporate executives would be chary of sharing their complete road map prospectively, since it would allow for pre-emptive action from competition. Second, they would feel rather silly if complete failure succeeds pompous pronouncements of savvy strategy. Hence, companies prefer that their strategy be ascribed to them when their success is obvious. Executives who have jumped the sinking ship discuss failed strategies—off-the-record and in hushed tones— or write about them in disguised form. Hence the pattern of decision-making that is implied in corporate strategy is, in reality, an external imposition made in retrospect, and most often in a rationalising manner.

This view is further strengthened by the view that most theories of and about orgnisational behaviour comprise either a priori propositions that can at best be said to have come from

Table 3.1: Competitive tools and their merits

S. no.	Competitive strength	Positive points	Risks	Requisites
1	Patents/Copyrights	Global, Unchallenged validity and total monopoly	Complacency, Discovery of side effects and contingent liabilities	Strong R&D ability to scale up marketing during currency of patents
2	Tying up critical resources (RM, distribution, etc.)	Near-monopoly, Cost advantage	Substitute RM or Alternate distribution channels	Early entry, Large resources for tying up
3	Product positioning and Segmentation	Can be done without too much material validity, Large customer acceptance in chosen segment	Tends to be iffy, someone else could position similarly and hijack customer base	Large market research and media budgets
4	Niche marketing	Near-monopoly in the niche, Strong brand equity created	Limited market size, 'Pigeon-holing' of the company in public mind	Significant research in use conditions and product development
5	Switching costs	Consumer loyalty enforced	Restricts versatility of product application	Product R&D for choosing switching cost

(contd.)

Table 3.1: contd.

S. no.	Competitive strength	Positive points	Risks	Requisites
6	Sound cost-quality profile	Usually the most reliable and durable strength; Creates sound reputation	Must restrict margins and, hence, RoI; Continuous product improvement to keep a winning profile	A long-term vision and commitment to business
7	Price-cutting	Wins short-term sales, may generate high volumes	Cuts into profits, Forces compromise on quality	Lean overheads and other fixed expenses
8	Long credit periods	May generate sales, keep business going	Cuts into margins	Large working capital

everyday observation, or are based on studies of compliant organisations. Or else they must be based on a 'revealed preference' approach. By very definitions, scholars and researchers can only be sure of what they have seen, or rather what they have been shown; and they may only see anything about corporate behaviour, if the concerned organisation allows them to see it. Organisations that are secretive or shy usually do not allow people to write about them and, hence, scholars end up over-studying organisations that permit access to their executives, data and facilities. People thus study universities, hospitals, public service organisations, and public sector companies because these are relatively open and transparent. They also study very few private sector organisations that are run by executives who find it socially impossible to deny entry and access to the insistent scholar. Some theories come when successful and reputed executives write on their experience in retrospect. How much do we know in the sense of documented knowledge, for instance, about plain, ordinary *marwari* business or about Chinese business firms? We know even less about firms that have an ill repute for economic offences. Thus in general a degree of humility is needed when one asserts the propositions in organisation theory and certainly theory of corporate strategy. Sadly, humility appears to be a rare virtue.

That said; let me return to the topic of assessment of corporate strategy. Business strategy involves goals in the market-place, ways of reaching them, financing the operations, manning the required roles and concerned organisational strategy of training, motivation, control, etc. First, let us look at the market performance. Assuming that the firm had formulated its goals after serious analysis, the most stringent ex-post assessment test would be to compare the performance with the goals. Hypothetically, let us say that Telco set the goal of selling five lakh cars (all models together) between 1998 and 2003. How many has it ended up selling by end of 2003 would really determine how sound its strategy was. Though stringent, this assessment criterion is perhaps a shade unrealistic. This assessment could be unrealistic because, in part, the behaviour of the markets is governed by factors of which some are unpredictable (South Asian meltdown, Kargil War, Gulf War, earthquakes) and some are dependent on the Government stand (duties on second hand cars, price of diesel, rates of taxes on cars of different size, rate of depreciation, policy on consumer finance). All goals of this kind are based on an estimation of the market potential, and then the assessment as to how much of the market potential the company would be able to achieve. Market potential is estimated on the basis of economic projections. This means that, perhaps, Telco would have projected the rate of growth of the economy, relative prices of diesel and petrol, demographic and income growth of the upper middle class segments, etc. Suppose, based on all this, the car market was assessed at 1.5 million pieces during this five-year period. Then, five lakhs cars amount to a 33 per cent market-share. Since Maruti Udyog Limited (MUL), Hyundai, India Motors, Honda, Ford and so on, all are attempting to grab a share in the same market, Telco management should be considered to have succeeded if it has captured close to such a market-share, even if the total market size did not grow to 1.5 million cars.

Such assessment is also unproductive because it can only result in conclusions such as, 'Telco management was very sound'— conclusions that have little instructional value. Students of business need to know the operational strategy of things like product features, product quality, product positioning, promotion, pricing, logistics, customer support through service centers, etc.; which of these things worked and which could have been done better? We have tried ex-post assessment to draw some lessons.

More crucial is the assessment ex-ante. When done, ex-ante (before the strategy is actually operational) such assessment is helpful to fine-tune the proposed strategy.

SWOT Analysis

The well-known SWOT—Strength, Weakness, Opportunities, Threats—approach is a useful tool for carrying out ex-ante assessment in a certain sphere. In *each of the areas*, one may identify the strengths of the company in question, its weaknesses, the opportunities opened up by these strengths and due to market behaviour, and the threats from economic and competitive behaviour that may make some of its action infertile. Let us look at one area—say, customer support—and carry on this hypothetical assessment purely for an illustrative purpose.

Customer support in terms of service centers, presumes basic durability of components, availability of spares, network of well-trained service centres and ease of maintenance outside authorised service centres. One may like to look at density of service centres (that might be reflected in average distance between two closest service centres) as well as load per service centre (both from the point of its viability and the point of speed of servicing to customers). How did Telco fare, ex-ante in 1998?

- It had a large number of well spread out, authorised service centres for the maintenance of its commercial vehicles as well as MUVs: a strength.
- It had a large number of stockists and retailers selling spares in most parts, again, for the commercial vehicles and MUV: another strength.
- The MUV were in the market and, hence, some non-authorised service centres would have come up for them: a possible strength.
- But many of these had training, facilities, locations, rapport, etc. with average middle class car buyers: an area of weakness and, hence, of action for fine-tuning.
- The service centres were known for maintaining rugged vehicles in which less finesse and delicacy was involved. If they carried that approach to cars, customers would be disturbed—and the decor-conscious customers would shy away from Telco cars: a potential weakness, hence an action point.
- MUL had a much longer and wider presence in the country as far as cars were concerned. It had a well-established network, remember their ad? A sure weakness vis-à-vis MUL and, hence, a threat of losing customers to MUL...and so on.

A similar analysis will be needed for product features, positioning, etc. All such analysis has become folklore of marketing courses and we need not spend more time on it.

Assessment of other aspects of strategy is less straightforward and involves greater situation-specific analysis and judgement. Such ex-ante assessment must address four crucial questions:

- Is the formulated strategy comprehensive in that it provides for all environmental factors?

- Is the formulated strategy internally consistent?
- Does the formulated strategy lend itself to implementation within the overall resources that can be accessed; and pose risks and negative consequences that can be absorbed by the firm?
- Does the formulated strategy agree with value orientations of the senior management and compatible with expectations and aspirations of the organisation members?

Comprehensive Understanding of the Environment

An environment scan is expected to precede strategy formulation. Environment scanning involves finding relevant features of the environment. Take the situation of a company considering entering/expanding its business in white goods in India. The company would do an environment scan: It would identify, for instance:

- Different products in the category (washing machines, refrigerators, kitchen appliances etc.)
- Variation and range in size and features
- Product use conditions and their compatibility with product design
- Existing competitors
- Key raw materials and components, terms of trade and important suppliers
- Marketing channels and trade practices in vogue
- Pricing trends in critical raw materials, components and final products
- Tax regime
- Consumer finance schemes
- Relationship between consumer financers and manufacturers
- Other important features pertaining to supply chain
- Demand drivers
- Promotional themes and marketing mix of competitors

When such information is compiled, the company would be in a position to claim that it understands the features of the environment. It is a good practice to be humble and believe that a single company can usually not alter the environment too much in the short run but must adjust to it. Hence the strategy devised by the company in the thematic areas related to the above features, would have to be realistically compatible with these environmental realities. If the proposed strategy deviates too much from any one of the critical features, the company must have adequate reasons to do so; and the management must be convinced about it. This is not to imply that only me-too behaviours are prudent—not in the least. This is only to say that flagrant neglect of critical variables in the environment is not justifiable. For instance,

- A water purifier like *Aquaguard* requires continuous, flowing water and stable electric supply for this product to be used. It would be heroic to introduce *Aquaguard* in cities where this is not available.
- Small-wheeled vehicles on rough, pot-hole-rich rural roads make a bad fit; and, hence, a company that tries to make this match has not done its homework.
- A company that tries to market GPRS (Global Positioning Record System) with a voice interface, to guide car drivers in India, when elementary cartographic maps for most cities are not available, is again asking for trouble.
- An institute that focuses on training highly skilled graduates for a market that does not wish to pay the price for the quality it gets has got a bad environmental fit.

Internal Consistency

This concept has been explained earlier in the note on concept of strategy. Assessment of strategy on the front of internal consistency must proceed with breaking down the overall strategic intent into proposed action on individual action fronts; assessing, from environmental assessment, the implications of these on other decision areas, and checking whether the proposals on those are compatible with requirement. To illustrate:

- If selling cars nationwide requires presence of well-trained service centres, and if the existing service centres lack equipment and training; then the strategy must also include a component that addresses the same. An absence of this component would generate internal inconsistency.

- If participative methodology is deemed to be essential for more effective management education, and if this requires students to work in groups; then, not making residential requirement obligatory and hence, creating adequate residential facilities for students generates internal inconsistency for a management institute.
- If it is proposed that market-share be captured through a push approach, and this requires large inventories at retail level, quick replenishment and fast servicing; then, not providing for large working capital to finance the trade inventories generates internal inconsistency for an FMCG company.

Risk and Resources

All business action eventually translates itself into positive or negative cash flows. Sadly, except when raising debts or occasional bouts of equity, positive cash flows succeed negative cash flows, and there is much larger uncertainty about them. Hence, it is better to assess ex-ante, the maximum negative cash flow and see if it can be managed with resource mobilisation efforts. Thus cash-flow statements need to be made for the period starting from the date of project initiative till the date of hitting peak sales. This alone will tell one, ex-ante, if the strategy can be implemented within the resource availability. Risk implications are captured in this method only if one considers scenarios, rather than definitive figures for expected cash flow. Sensitivity analysis, etc. should be performed on key variables to build possible scenarios. It is, perhaps, also to important to calculate leverage values for each of the years in the period ex-ante, and confirm whether the implied level of risk is acceptable. More importantly, assessment of resource and risk implications can be instructive in preparing fallback options, contingency plans and exit strategy.

Value Compatibility

Questions of values might lurk in several decision areas. For instance, a joint venture with a foreign partner always brings in the possibility of eventual loss of control and may be a situation wherein one may be rendered irrelevant. This has been experienced by several Indian business houses. The eventual diminution of stature may not be acceptable to the management and, hence, the option of a joint venture can be said to raise the question of compatibility with values. Value compatibility may also become relevant in matters such as concerns for quality and assumption of responsibility of product performance post-sale, about the level of risk that the business poses, about the nature of products and the consuming class, even about the nature of product advertisements and so on. (Have you seen scantily clad women uttering *double entendre* in ads for Tata products? Does it have anything to do with values?)

A respectable business house may want to look at possible businesses that offer high cash and profit potential, but may balk at the implications of some of these lines (such as liquor) on the quality of interface with regulators and politicians. A conservative institute of learning may recognise the need to introduce co-educational and residential courses, but may feel very uncomfortable with the usual consequences of young people thus thrown together.

Not only do the values of senior management become important, it is the ordinary, existing staff members who could make things difficult for the management, if the requirements of the new strategy run counter to their aspirations or create a sense of outrage in them. I sat on the selection of faculty in one institute, when one male candidate was considered prima facie unacceptable, because he kept long hair which was tied at the back, with the unassailable argument: 'all of us in the staff would become a laughing stock if such a person is inducted into the institute.' He was brilliant in his subject and the subject represented a new foray. But if the man was not acceptable, there was no way one could get going with the new line. With the news that an enzyme, rennet, was used to manufacture a dairy product and that it was extracted from the intestines of a calf, there was tremendous pressure on the management to simply stop the production—and the pressure came from within the organisation itself.

Chapter Four

INGREDIENTS OF THE SUCCESS FORMULAE

During 1997–99, I researched 10 'exceptional' business firms that had started in the small industry mode and had achieved exceptional success. They have become shining examples of brilliant corporate performance. The list then included Bicon, Mastek, Orchid, Dr Reddy's Laboratories and Sun Pharmaceuticals among others. These companies have continued to do well during the period subsequent to the publication of my book based on that research. Later, in 2000–02, I researched the pattern of response of Indian businesses to the changes in the economic environment in India during the Nineties. That research gave me an opportunity to study patterns of decision-making associated with successful coping mechanisms, that helped the companies thrive even during adverse economic conditions. I use these two researches to draw lessons on good performance. In the next chapter, I present patterns of decision-making that seem to be associated with an inability to cope with changes in the environment, poor performance, stagnation and sickness. Hopefully, a combination of the positive suggestions, in this chapter, and the tips about what to avoid, given in the next chapter will together prove to be of practical utility to managers. The theme of opportunism and strategic behaviour is picked up in the last chapter, again, where I explore the basic patterns of decision-making that facilitate or hinder such decisions.

Choice of Products

I find it both instructive and obvious that a company that chooses a product (and a mission in general) that is in the growth phase of its product life-cycle (PLC), seems to be able to achieve better growth and performance. I drew this lesson from the research that I did on the exceptionally successful small-scale industries. Nine of the 10 companies that I then studied had grown and continued to grow, because they repeatedly introduced and chose products that were either new in India or were, at any rate, in the growth phase of their PLC. Some initiated the product category in India. For instance, Sumangal Prakashan started the new product category of calendar plus almanac through their *Kalnirnaya*. Biocon was perhaps the first to start the manufacture of the enzyme that was used to stone-wash denim in India. Praj Industries grew with the popular adoption of the continuous fermentation process equipment they introduced in India. Flex Industries had a runaway success, initially, on the back of its flexible packing machinery; developed and introduced by them as the new packing medium in the mid-Eighties. (That Flex tripped later, is a different story). Flat Products grew rapidly when it caught the trend of the metal rolling industry, towards high-width and high speed rolling. The choice of product helped it do well even in a hopelessly depressed industrial machinery sector in the Nineties.

It is fairly obvious that if one is among the first to introduce a product in its growth cycle and the product clicks in the market, then one would grow with the product. Yet, this by itself does not guarantee long-term performance nor performance during bad times. As a recent book[1] points out, no business can keep doing well eternally, on the back of just one or two products. Choosing and introducing a new product (or, the next best thing, a product at the growth phase of its PLC) will sustain the firm and help it grow for a while. Then, it will stagnate. It must keep adding new products to its portfolio just to sustain the higher level of business. And, if it wants the growth itself to be a continuous phenomenon,

---

[1] Baghai, M; Coley, S; and White, D; *The Alchemy of Growth*, Oxford University Press, New Delhi, 2000.

then the products it adds to its portfolio must each be new or in the growth phase of their respective PLC. This book then goes on to talk of three horizons: embryonic, emerging and mature; reflecting the phased manner in which the various products in the total portfolio will start accelerating and sustaining the growth. Continuous addition of products at the growth phase of their PLC is very difficult to achieve. In the first place, it presumes that the firm can identify such products. This requires that someone in the management has far-sightedness and a deep understanding of the way the world is moving. Second, it requires an ability to quickly design an appropriate product—which means creative and productive design abilities. Finally, the firm must have the ability to grow through the entire routine of new product introduction (product testing, test marketing, launch and scaling up). The combination of such abilities is rare. In India, Dr Reddy demonstrated this combination. I recommend to industry-watchers to try and plot the development, trial and full-blown marketing of various products (starting, perhaps, with Metronudizole, through Sulphamethaxazole, Methyldopa, Quinolones and so on, till the recent Nimsulide led growth) that gave his firms phenomenal growth over the last 20 years or so, so as to fully appreciate the point made above.

The relative roles of the 'management' and the 'professionals' in this process are, perhaps, quite different from those in the business of a firm that sticks to just one fairly unchanging product for decades. The Birlas, for example, have shown how to manage the latter type of business: rayon, cement, aluminium, etc. The basic product has a long life-cycle. Its market continues to grow at least demographically, or with the economy. In such a business, the focus shifts to management of scale, working towards mastering the technology for achieving cost positions, achieving a control on the market and so on; aspects quite different from those involved in continuously introducing new products. Sure these businesses worked in the era when complex regulations made both, setting up a new industrial unit or introduction of a wholly new product in the existing unit, tedious. Yet, it is worth pondering whether the family business finds it easy to stick to commodity-like products for decades and, if so, why? Also, to think about why technocrats or at least first generation entrepreneurs take the route of ever new products for growth.

Efficiency in Operations

The first and perhaps a central lesson drawn from the research on corporate response to economic changes, is the importance of operational efficiency in achieving sustained sound performance. Importance of efficiency is obvious. However, this is the age of cynicism. People tend to ignore the obvious. Businessmen and companies come in all sizes and shapes. I have personally witnessed many conversations in which businessmen derides painstaking, hard work; stating that the resultant efficiency will earn perhaps a paisa or two. He argues that spending the same time in managing the regulator, instead, or devising some smart tricks in the market, may produce as many as a 100 rupees.

It is, in some sense, reassuring to note that efficiency in operations achieved through some good management and a lot of hard work is still associated with sound performance and lasting success. Yet, I want to point out that the drive towards efficiency is rare enough to become remarkable. Generally, there is a pressure on the management either during the expansion phase of a company or during the time when the external environment is becoming tough, sluggish or competitive. Efficiency tends to take a backseat. That is why this drive towards efficiency is even more remarkable. Before I explore reasons for this lesson, let me give some illustrations for the same.

Table 4.2 and Table 4.3 sum up the difference between sound performers who coped with difficult economic changes in the wake of liberalisation, and those who faltered and lost ground. Both, the sound performers and those who faltered, have been chosen sector-wise to eliminate the effect of the sector. The judgements summed up in these tables are based on changes in the appropriate, financial ratios for the companies during the period 1993–99. The sample size for each sector has been around 12, half of which were chosen from sound performers. These ratios demonstrate superior operating efficiency of successful businesses and the sound performers who weathered the stormy Nineties.[2]

A movement towards faster turnover ratios, shorter working capital cycles, lower cost of production and hence bigger gross

---

[2] *Annex 1* gives the necessary details of the research methodology for the scholastic-minded readers.

margin, improvement in productivity, etc. by the better performing companies, across the sectors in a hostile environment, clearly
demonstrates the importance of the efforts to improve operating
efficiency. Rather than blandly admiring the fact that efficiency is
associated with superior performance, it is important to see what
possible steps lead to that operational efficiency. One can piece
together the response of successful business units only by identifying these steps. Only then can one learn something really useful.

Two factors lead to superior product margins. The first is the
fact that poor performing companies used, or were forced to use,
larger than usual price discounts as a competitive tool to keep
their market-shares. The second factor is that the better performers
had high-value products in their portfolios or they introduced the
same. The poor performers chose, or had to continue with, the
low-end products. Choice of products and hence the mission can
help a business get better operating margins. That can explain
how the better performing companies are able to record and
improve their gross margins in a more competitive environment
while the gross margins for the poor performers keep falling. Our
investigations reveal that both the phenomena are operative. In
fact, choosing low-end, me-too products and selling them using
price discounts and longer credit period is a commonly adopted
business style; usually of the old, family businesses in India. Well-
chosen, high-value products sold on the USP (unique selling
proposition) of high quality and performance clearly seem to help
companies do better.

When we see better performing companies having superior
inventory turnover ratios, we need to ask why they are able to do
it. These ratios suggest better logistics management, brought
about by efforts to shift from 'just in case' to 'just in time'.

A complex set of inter-related acts can achieve huge efficiency gains. As I wrote earlier, usually during the growth phase,
there is less attention to operational efficiencies. But this need not
always be so. For example, let us look at. Core Parenterals Ltd.,
a company that achieved runaway success in the IV fluid market
in the early Nineties. During the course of its phenomenally fast
expansion during 1988–92, Core was also focusing on continuous
and sustained improvement of its operations. Despite the Gulf
War and the consequent oil shock, a runway inflation of the early
Nineties and other such external factors, Core actually reduced the

real cost of raw materials, per unit, during the same time. The drop in unit costs came not because of capacity expansion alone, but also because of painstaking efforts by a technically-oriented top manager who focused on operating efficiency.

Efficiency is enhanced also by the choice of operating methods. Outsourcing can sometimes help some companies improve their operational efficiencies. In fact, prior to the Nineties, the dominant corporate trend was essentially to 'contractualise' labour jobs. There was a sort of game going on, between the business world and a very pro-labour judiciary. The former kept increasing the permanent liabilities of the management towards the workforce and the latter kept devising newer ways of distancing at least a part of the labour force from the organisation. But the Nineties saw the onset of the tendency to outsource. It possibly began with the pharma industry, where getting drugs made by third party factories began in a big way. This way of operations increases the proportion of variable costs in the total costs, reduces risks and makes exit easier. This also automatically helps to bring about a massive increase inventory turnover. The focal firm needs to hold stock in its account only when it is to be marketed, and can avoid holding stock of raw material, etc.

Debtor turnover was also sought to be increased particularly in the pharma industry at first, and, later, in most other lines. This was done by increasing price discounts, but insisting on either spot payments or very short credit periods. The trade innovation of appointing intermediaries who would finance trade stocks and credits against higher commissions also occurred around this time. In fact, smaller pharma companies began using the newly emerging service of the 'propaganda cum distribution' (PCD) agencies that took over much of the functions of the field sales force.

In summary, high operating efficiencies are associated with superior coping with bad times and with superior performance. They come from a range of actions on several fronts.

Innovation in Operating Technology and Systems

By technology, I do not mean elaborate nuts and bolts, complicated circuits or horrendous codes. Operating technology to me is, simply, your way of doing things. Most industries have a somewhat patterned way of doing things. Competing companies source materials, process them, seek out clients, woo them, etc. in a somewhat similar manner. This is how they find it so easy to absorb the people they poach from each other. An innovation essentially means introducing a variation in this patterned way of doing things. So far, no one else has tried it and this may be for the better. In this sense, multi-level marketing is an innovation in operating technology to push high-value personal products, compared to the conventional way of distribution and marketing. I think that innovation in operating technology is an important element that helps companies cope with a competitive environment, win business and make profits. I offer some examples.

Development of software in India for clients located in USA, has been the major source of business for the IT industry for the last 15 years or so. In the old days, software codes were written in India, then copied on to spools, taken to the clients' mainframe computers, installed, debugged and applied there by the company's staff. The element of personal interaction with client machines and client staff was important in the process. Nowadays, the client's needs are communicated over the net to the development group, which, in turn, works on the problems and communicates the solution via the net as well. In theory, the two could work together for years without having to see each other. This is just like the system of using travel agents who book your air tickets and whom you pay periodically. You do not have to see their faces, at least not to conduct the business, I mean. This is the change in operating technology.

Satyam was the first company to make this change come through, though not easily. Its clients, in the early Nineties, could not believe the possibility of working entirely from a distance. Nor was Satyam such a big name then. So the innovation involved working out the solution in USA itself, but away from the client's site, communicating it over the slowly emerging net, debugging it through email interaction with the client staff and, thus, demonstrating that this could be done without face-to-face, personal interaction. Having done this for one company—John Deere to be precise, Satyam could then convincingly argue that the distance between the development site and the user site ceased to matter once the communication occurred over the net. Satyam calls this, 'The Little India Experiment'. This is how the terms on-site, on-shore but off-site, and off-site and off-shore emerged in the IT industry. To back its new operating technology, Satyam invested quite substantially in communications hardware.

Another example is the remarkably innovative approach to marketing adopted by Sun, when it was a small and insignificant company in the pharmaceutical industry.[3] With the assistance of knowledgeable therapy experts, Sun would identify the latest and, perhaps, highly coveted books or articles at the 'cutting edge', obtain reprints or reprint rights and send them periodically and repeatedly to the practitioners of the particular therapy. This helped Sun build an image as a company that prized professional excellence. Sun also initiated the whole concept of continuing education for professionals and reinforced this very same image. The real point is that Sun did this when, and probably because, it had virtually no other major competitive strength to fall back on.

Undoubtedly, an innovation in operating technology is copied very quickly by others. Today software development and communicating with the client over the net, in the process, has become a standard practice and is no longer Satyam's competitive edge. Similarly, many pharmaceutical companies have copied the theme of professional excellence and offered continuing education. Those who emulate perhaps introduce improved variations on that theme. But then, each innovation is copied sooner or later. The fact that it is copied, demonstrates its soundness and appeal. Also, just because an innovation will be copied does not render this strategy ineffectual. After all, Satyam won important software work through this innovation even when its IT prowess was weak compared to established names such as Tata Consultancy Service or others at that time. Similarly, Sun won a great deal of business and vastly improved its market standing by using the approach discussed above. An innovation in operating technology certainly benefits the company for a while. The company must take advantage of this and move on before the advantage withers away.

Competitive Edge Based on Bootstrapping

Let us look at some specific examples. In a hopelessly unattractive vegetable oil industry, a company called Sudha Oil Industries

---

[3] Phansalkar, SJ; *Making Growth Happen* (See the case description on Sun), Response Books, New Delhi, 1999.

has shown remarkable improvement in the sheer efficiency of operations. Its plant utilisation is far superior to that of other comparable units. By making appropriate arrangements with bran suppliers in the huge rice growing tracts of Andhra Pradesh, Chhattisgarh and Orissa, it is able to extend plant utilisation. By introducing sound practises for raw material grading, it can segregate the many lots of raw materials. It can thus get rice bran of differing degrees of rancidity and, hence, can actually sell some of it as branded edible oil at far higher prices. Most other rice bran units sell the oil mainly to soap makers. Sudha is among the few oil units that have achieved complete vertical integration. The company has processes not only for oil extraction rightdown to refining and hydrogenation, but has also gone up to the stage of extracting fatty acids distillates and bottling of oxygen, all in single locale. Sudha Oil also experimented with undertaking soyabean operations on its own, found it too working-capital intensive and lost no time in wet leasing of its facilities which were conveniently located close to a port. Most tellingly, perhaps, it has abstained from linking manufacturing operations with speculative trade in oil commodities. When one pictures the stages of processing in the oil industry, the distribution of industry units could perhaps be somewhat like this:

Total units	1000
Stand alone expeller units	650
Expeller units + solvent extraction	150
Expeller + solvent extraction (SE) + refining	90
Expeller + SE + refining + hydrogenation	85
Expeller + SE + refining + hydrogenation + fatty acid distillates	20
The above + bottling of oxygen, a by-product in hydrogenation stage	5

Seldom, if ever, has there been any unit that has started with all stages built in from the word go. Clearly, this is too capital intensive. Yet, it is also not very common to see units generally progressing in this direction. There are interesting and instructive reasons for abstaining from the obviously beneficial strategy of integration. In the first place, edible oil industry is notorious for its ethical standards, both in terms of product quality and in terms of its tax compliance. This puts a premium on facelessness and a discount on becoming visible in any sense. So, not too much 'formal' surplus is generated. If you get to see the books of an edible oil company, you will find them quite rickety. One also observes a rather common tendency to deploy the resources generated for speculative acquisition of raw material stocks or, these days, for import of palm oil; rather than in continuous technology upgradation and vertical acquisition. Such tendencies indicate the strong prevalence of short-term, opportunistic, mercantile capitalist attitudes in the concerned industrialists. Sudha's vertical integration and drive towards operating efficiencies comes as a sharp and pleasant contrast to the general pattern of the oil industry.

Proactive Behaviour

As per the simple model in Chapter one, a firm receives a trigger from its task environment. Depending on the way the management interprets it and manages to steer it through the maze of the organisation dynamics, it makes a response in terms of changes in some aspect of its business behaviour. *If the firm is able to detect the signs of the change 'in the air', takes these signs seriously and makes changes in its behaviour anticipating the change before it has actually happened, it is purely proactive.* Such foresight may be quite rare. *On the other hand, if the firm tries to pull on with its frozen behaviour as long as possible despite the fact that the changes have actually taken place, and it modifies its business behaviour only to the barest minimum extent; we call it a reactive firm.* The difference between the two lies in the timing of the decision and its motivation. Proactive decision-making is ahead or along with the change, and is made without being forced under the threat for well-being or survival. Reactive decisions are definitely made after the changes have happened and, usually, when all efforts of the type described by Merton (see Chapter one) have failed to remove or reduce the threat caused by the change.

We asked the firms what changes they made in their business behaviour during the decade of the Nineties. Questions were put forth about behaviour in all functional areas: marketing, finance, production and logistics, quality, governance and so on. We analysed the behaviour on the proactive-reactive continuum. Magnitude of behaviour changes, their qualitative contents and timing of the decision determined the locus the firm on this continuum. We also related this behaviour with the performance of the firm. The results were remarkable. They are presented in Table 4.1.

Table 4.1: Proactive-reactive continuum and performance

Attribute	Number of companies that coped successfully and performed well	Number of companies that faltered
Proactive in product-market	10	2
Neutral on product-market and in logistics and organisation matters	4	0
Reactive in product-market and proactive on other dimensions	1	0
Neutral on product-market and reactive on others	0	6
Reactive in product-market and reactive on others	0	7
Total	15	15

Source: Phansalkar and Mardikar, 2002.

Annex 1 to this chapter gives the details of definitions and parameters used, while coming to the above conclusions. The results are truly remarkable. Ten of the 15 companies that were rated as sound performers were seen as being proactive in the product-market arena. Only one company managed to do well, despite being reactive in the product-market arena. It did so because it was exceptionally proactive on the logistic front. Thirteen of the 15 poor performers were seen as reactive: seven of these were reactive in product-market arena and the remaining were reactive in others areas. The data is sufficiently suggestive of the positive relationship between proactive behaviour and sound performance. In particular, it appears that the proactive behaviour in the product-market arena is the most important factor influencing a good performer. It is also clear that reactive behaviour in general, and reactive behaviour in product-market arena in particular, makes it difficult for the firm to do well. While I think the association between proactive behaviour and sound performance is clear, I believe there are three issues to be explored and understood well.

Circularity

The first is in exploring whether a proactive firm achieves good performance, or whether good performance of a firm enables it to take a proactive stance for the subsequent years. One can certainly argue for both. I, of course, have been arguing that a proactive firm is likely to achieve sound performance even in a hostile environment. Yet it can be argued that sound performance provides both, the confidence in one's ability and judgment to a management; and that, in turn, encourages them to take proactive decisions. In the evolutionary existence of a business firm, it is difficult to pinpoint which comes first. While I do not have evidence to assert the direction of this relationship, I am tempted to argue that proactive behaviour is as much a function of the resources and track record of performance as of the basic mindset of the men and women at the helm. Hence, proactive behaviour can be viewed as an antecedent rather than a consequence of performance.

What Makes a Firm Proactive

I offer some tentative explanations based on observations during the process of our research. In the first place, the men and women at the helm of affairs ought to be committed to the business, ought to be deriving pride from it and identifying with it. If the business remains merely a means of earning a livelihood or a lifestyle, while the men at the helm of affairs derive their identity from some other walk of life (cricket, paintings, social service or politics, just to name a few commonly observed passions), then it is unlikely they will take extraordinary interest in the growth and performance of the company they run. They certainly desire that the company runs reasonably well and earns them the money they need. Hence they may perhaps take serious interests only when things start turning bad. Yet as long as they get their sustenance, they may not worry too much. Second, they must be willing to share control with at least a few 'professionals' who not only share their passion for the growth and sound performance of the company, but also bring in industry experience, understanding of the business and, in part, an entrepreneurial drive. By the same token, if they do not share such a control on the way things are done in the company, then they will limit the scope of company behaviour to their own limited competence. One may then see parts of the company changing, adapting and improving while the other parts become a drag on it. I have no intention to stretch this particular point nor do I wish to run anyone down. But the evidence we got in our research suggests that stand-alone companies seem to be more likely to exhibit proactive behaviour than companies that are part of a 'group'—whether owned by a family or otherwise. A stand-alone company is likely to be young and led by a promoter whose entrepreneurial zeal is vibrant. He does not find any inhibitions in taking such decisions as he and his 'core group' of managers deem necessary. There is no baggage of history to be managed. He must manage only few, if any, sensitive egos. He experiences no constraints of ensuring parity between 'different units in the group'. He is thus relatively unconstrained and free. A pro-moter manager in the situation of a family business or a group of companies has all these problems. Sometimes the problem can be compounded, if the proactive behaviour is associated with genera-tional transition in the 'family'. The younger man who has taken over from the old patriarch has probably grown up in business under the loving care of some of the senior men in the core group. Having ascended to the throne and having judged that proactive behaviour in product, logistics, organisation or other matters is absolutely essential for the companies to shake off the old rust and become dynamic again, he now must negotiate with all these old people. Perhaps he must encounter statements like, 'Had *Babuji* been alive, he would not do this'. Tact, diplomacy, a surgeon's knife, etc. could be some of the tools he must deploy. Finally, the promoters themselves personally must be moderate risk takers. Further, by design of the organisational culture, the people work-ing in it ought to be willing to experiment, take risks and try out new things. If failures are hit with a double whammy, initiative will be stifled and proactive behaviour may recede.

Caveats to Proactive Behaviour

Proactive behaviour, by itself, is not adequate. In fact, one must differentiate between deliberate and proactive behaviour of a committed and serious businessman, and the sheer opportunism found so commonly across the spectrum of Indian business. En-tering a new field that has opened up early on, is sure a sign of proactive behaviour. But doing it in a dilettante manner, without due thought about the synergies and shared strength between the extant business and the new line, without any evidence of due thought and analysis of its financial implications, etc. may amount to sheer opportunism. One has seen so many such ventures, set up purely with the hope that in a medium term future, someone will buy the venture at a profitable price. This is more of treasury opportunism than proactive behaviour. Even when the firm behaves proactively as distinguished from banal opportunism, there still are some caveats. These pertain to financial risks and leveraging. For example, the flexible packaging innovator, Flex, acted proactively and set up huge facilities to manufacture Bi-axially Oriented Poly-Propylene (BOPP) and other packaging materials. It did so by managing to obtain large loans from financial institutions. So brilliant was its performance till the time of sanctioning the loan, that it could really persuade the bankers to part with the money. Subsequent events made the plans go awry: industry plunged into recession, the company could simply not raise the business levels enough to smoothly absorb the debt-servicing burden; and the company also lost some of its political clout. What remains is a debris of a grandiose plan. Scores of such examples are to be seen in several industries in the late Nineties. Thus, proactive behaviour in product-market arena as well as in terms of investment in logistics must be matched by financial prudence for a sound performance in the medium to long.

Teamwork

This point is often repeated by all the pundits and, hence, I shall not belabour it much. I shall only argue that my research has shown that the companies that did well during the decade of the Nineties, as well as those others who have shown very sound performance, had attempted to put teamwork in practise. Naturally, all companies claim that they follow a team rather than hierarchical style of functioning. In some industries, notably the knowledge and the creative industries, this becomes a must. Yet one finds that, in reality, the spirit of teamwork is missing in a whole range of companies managed in the traditional style. The business world is growing increasingly complex and promoters need the inputs of competent colleagues simply because they are no longer competent enough to understand these complexities. Simultaneously, the proportion of professionally qualified people in the management cadre is rising; and a lot of these people find it difficult to be doers, without being contributors to the process of deciding what is to be done. Thus business realities as well as managers' outlooks now demand the shift in working style, in favour of teamwork. Yet, the values of paternalistic hierarchy do not wither away as easily as that. This is thus a crucial conflict, a clash of cultures; and one that affects the business fortunes of those who would not change.

Transparency and Systematisation

Teamwork generally leads to greater transparency; at least within the team and, often, a general rise in transparency follows. Second, good governance is now more or less accepted as a desirable norm in the industrial circles. In my research, I found that companies that showed high performance were generally those who followed elaborate formalisation in systems, mainly to further transparency and good governance. One can see the link, though perhaps a bit indirect one, between this and performance. Sound performance of a durable type comes from consistent improvement in products and services as well as consistent efforts towards making operations more efficient. These three features have tended to override smart accounting, speculation and sharp use of legal loopholes as prime sources of good financial performance that prevailed hitherto. Clearly, transparency and systematisation are more associated with the former attributes and may actually hinder the latter three. The choice rests with managements.

Readers will find most of the above ingredients in the case of the company presented at the end of this chapter.

Financing Decisions

I offer two highly summarized tables that show how the decisions of better performing companies differed from those that faltered on some key operating and financial matters during the decade of the Nineties (see Tables 4.2 and 4.3).

Some features are to be noted from Table 4.3. In the first place, by shifting the composition of funds in favour of own funds, the better performing companies reduce cash outflows on account of interest payments. They also achieve greater stability through reduction in total leverage. Third, rather than fresh equity infusion, they rely on accruals as a source of funds. Finally, they seem to allocate it to financing the working capital needs. These are straightforward conclusions from the data in Table 4.3.

Table 4.2: Comparison between high performers and poor performers in six sectors

	Indicators about operations	Indicators about financial structure	Indicators about efficiency
Drugs and Pharma	High performers show smaller costs of production and energy, higher marketing costs and more outsourcing.	High performers show higher current and quick ratio. They show smaller and falling debt equity ratios.	High performers are more efficient in terms of turning over raw materials, finished goods and debtors.
Plastic products	High performers show smaller and falling costs of production and higher outsourcing. They spent more on marketing.	No noteworthy differences.	High performers show higher efficiency in terms of raw materials turnover, finished goods turnover and debtor turnover.
Textile processing	High performers increased their outsourcing, had low energy costs in CGS, lower proportion of wage costs.	High performers had low debt-equity ratios though they rose during the period and registered big rise in operating leverage.	High performers show much superior turnover of raw materials and debtors and have a smaller working capital pipeline.
Computers and IT	Despite the importance of manpower, the proportion of manpower costs in costs of sales fell for high	No noteworthy differences, except that high performers have tended to become much more	High performers all have higher debtors' turnover ratios, though these are falling.

(contd.)

Table 4.2: contd.

	Indicators about operations	Indicators about financial structure	Indicators about efficiency
	performers. High performers registered a fall in marketing costs in CGS.	liquid and show higher quick ratio.	
Cement	Raw material cost as a proportion of cost of production fell for high performers but grew for low performers. Energy and distribution costs rose faster for low performers.	High performers have very high financial leverage.	High performers show much higher raw material turnover but smaller finished goods turnover. High performers have smaller working capital cycles.
Industrial machinery	Cost of production as percentage of sales rose faster for low performers. Raw materials account for more in cost of production for high performers. Energy costs rose faster for low performers.	High performers have much smaller debt equity ratios. Their current and quick ratios are also smaller.	High performers are superior in terms of turn-over of raw materials and finished goods. Debtors' turnover has fluctuated widely. Working capital cycle for poor performers is much larger than for the high performers.

Source: Phansalkar and Mardikar, 'Weathering the Storm', report submitted to the ICICI Bank.

Table 4.3: Comparison on financial parameters

Attribute	Difference between companies that did well vis-à-vis the poor performers					
	Pharma	IT and computers	Plastic products	Textile processing	Industrial machinery	Cement
Debt-equity ratio (difference)	-0.71	-.24	No abs. diff, rise during decade for high performance	-1.1	-4.8	0.35
Leverage	Better performers reduced it sharply	Reduced for both the groups	Rose for both the groups	Rose for low performers	Rose for both, faster for poor performers	Marginal increase in both
Accruals as a proportion of total funds	56%	10%	No diff.	55%	49%	22%
% of total funds applied to working capital	48%	-29%	4%	23%	8%	-8%

N = 67

Source: Phansalkar and Maralkar, 'Weathering the Storm', report submitted to the ICICI Bank.

Annex 1

Methodology of the Research

A

This research was done in four phases. In the first phase, we used exports performance, sales performance and profit performance during the Nineties, to identify high and low performing industry sectors. For this purpose, compounded annual rates of growth in these parameters were calculated for individual companies in the sector, and then averaged for the sector. We chose four high performing sectors: pharmaceuticals, plastic products, textile processing and IT and computers; and two low performing sectors namely industrial machinery and cement. In the second phase, we used the same three parameters to identify high and poor performing companies within each of these sectors. Six of each type were chosen for each sector. Their financials were analysed and compared for the period of the Nineties.

The third phase comprised conducting a primary survey explained below. Finally, the fourth phase was preparation of case studies on 10 companies in these sectors.

B

How did we judge proactive or reactive behaviour?

We collected data on several aspects from 30 companies. Some aspects reflected mere cosmetic change, some reflected substantial change. We asked what the change was, and when was it introduced. The data is indicated below. The companies were classified as high performing if their CAGR in ROCE exceeded the average for the sample.

Table 4.4: Corporate behaviour regarding change of company name

S. no.	Attribute category	High performing	Low performing
1	Did not change the name of the company	14	10
2	Changes the name of company	1	5
	Total number	15	15

Table 4.4 is the cosmetic change in the name of the company. This was asked because Merton's model suggests that groups with a vested interest may make mere cosmetic change as well. This does not reflect any difference across performance category.

A company is seen as proactive if it introduced many new products and early on in the decade of the Nineties. See the data in Tables 4.5 and 4.6.

Table 4.5: Introduction of new products

S. no.	Attribute category	High performing	Low performing
1	Continuous introduction of new products, large number of total products introduced	10	0
2	Few (2–4) new products introduced	4	7
3	One new product or new application	1	5
4	No new products	0	3

Table 4.6: Year(s) when new products were introduced

S. no.	Attribute category	High performing	Low performing
1	All the time during the period	7	1
2	Before 1995	3	6
3	After 1995 or not at all	5	8

From Tables 4.5 and 4.6, it appears that superior performance is associated with early introduction of many products in this turbulent decade.

The way the new products are related to the existing product line also reflects on the attitude of the company. Related products, or products that indicate a vertical integration are rated as being more proactive in the same industry. The same holds true for re-positioning of the products as well as for the simultaneous introduction of substitutes. See Table 4.7.

Table 4.7: Relation of the new product to original products

S. no.	Attribute category	High performing	Low performing
1	A product in the nature of backward or forward integration	2	2
2	Re-positioning of the old product or line-widening	1	3
3	Substitute to the old product		2
4	Combination of the above	11	5
5	Unrelated or no new product	1	3

The way a company distributes the products has implications on inventory levels, net realisations as well as on outstanding debtors.

Table 4.8: Changes in distribution network

S. no.	Attribute category	High performing	Low performing
1	Changed the configuration	4	3
2	No change made current distribution system	11	12
3	C&F format	6	5
4	Company + dealers format	6	8
5	Ex-factory sales format	2	
6	Through agents		2
7	Franchises	1	

Table 4.9: Trade credits

S. no.	Attribute category	High performing	Low performing
1	Credit period increased	4	4
2	Credit period decreased	4	1
3	No change in current trade credit system	7	10
4	Cash or on sight	6	5
5	Others	9	10

Table 4.10: Change in overall production volume

S. no.	Attribute category	High performing	Low performing
1	Greatly increased (>>25%)	13	3
2	Increased (10–25%)	2	6
3	Flat (-10 – 10%)	0	4
4	Decreased (-10 – -25%)	0	2

Table 4.11: Steps to meet rising production demand and making new products

S. no.	Attribute category	High performing	Low performing
1	Building new factories	6	4
2	Acquiring factories of others	0	1
3	Sub-contracting production	1	
4	Multiple options used	6	
5	No action taken or needed	2	10

Table 4.12: Other changes in manufacturing to achieve increased capacity

S. no.	Attribute category	High performing	Low performing
1	De-bottlenecking	2	2
2	Additional lines	3	5
3	New factories/technology	5	3
4	Multiple options	4	0
5	None/Not applicable	1	5

Table 4.13: Location and timing of the new factories built

S. no.	Attribute category	High performing	Low performing
1	Existing location	3	6
2	New locations	9	5
3	Combinations	3	3
4	Before 1995	3	4
5	After 1995	7	2
6	Multiple years	5	5

Table 4.14: Extent of outsourcing of products/services

S. no.	Attribute category	High performing	Low performing
1	No outsourcing	5	9
2	Marginal outsourcing	4	3
3	Outsourcing of highly skilled tasks	1	1
4	Some processes outsourced	3	0
5	Significant outsourcing	2	2

Table 4.15: Changes in technology

S no.	Attribute category	High performing	Low performing
1	No change	5	6
2	Marginal changes	3	2
3	Significant changes	1	1
4	New equipment's	5	4
5	Others	1	2

Table 4.16: Sources of new technology

S. no.	Attribute category	High performing	Low performing
1	Original technology supplier	4	4
2	New, foreign suppliers	5	5
3	Own R&D	5	2
4	Not applicable	1	4

Table 4.17: Year in which new technology was adopted

S. no.	Attribute category	High performing	Low performing
1	Before 1995	4	1
2	After 1995	6	9
3	Not applicable	5	5

Table 4.18: Changes in factory layout made

S. no.	Attribute category	High performing	Low performing
1	None	6	11
2	Layouts changes	3	2
3	Some process flows modified	2	1
4	Others	1	0
5	Combination of these	3	1

Table 4.19: Change of supplier to self-certification for supplies

S. no.	Attribute category	High performing	Low performing
1	No supplier so changed	7	5
2	Some supplier changed	5	8
3	Key suppliers changed	2	1
4	All suppliers changed	0	1
5	Not applicable	1	0

Table 4.20: Adoption of TQM and ISO

S. no.	Attribute category	High performing	Low performing
1	TQM adopted	5	1
2	ISO or equivalent implemented in more than 50% plants/units	12	6
3	Under implementation	1	1
4	Year of implementation before 1995	4	2
5	Year of implementation after 1995	9	5
6	Not applicable	2	8

Table 4.21: Extent of automation

S. no.	Attribute category	High performing	Low performing
1	Accounts and HR records computerised	4	8
2	Accounts, HR, factories systems and marketing computerised	4	5
3	ERP adopted	3	1
4	Ecom readiness claimed	4	1

Table 4.22: Changes made in organisation

S. no.	Attribute category	High performing	Low performing
1	Organisation structure changed	13	8
2	Current structure is functional	4	11
3	Current structure is divisional	3	3
4	Current structure is matrix form	2	1
5	SBU pattern adopted	4	0
6	Combination	2	0

Table 4.23: Involvement of external agency in restructuring

S. no.	Attribute category	High performing	Low performing
1	External agency involved	4	1
2	External agency not involved	11	14

Table 4.24: New senior management roles created

S. no.	Attribute category	High performing	Low performing
1	No new roles	2	8
2	Functional roles	1	2
3	General management roles	8	4
4	SBU Head type roles	4	1

Table 4.25: Composition of the board

S. no.	Attribute category	High performing	Low performing
1	No change	8	9
2	Senior managers inducted	2	1
3	Outside non-executive directors inducted	4	3
4	Combination of 2 and 3	1	2

Table 4.26: Size of employment

S. no.	Attribute category	High performing	Low performing
1	Employment of workforce actually increased	13	10
2	Need for workforce reduction recognized	8	10
3	Need for workforce reduction not recognized	1	1
4	No comment about need for workforce reduction	6	4

Table 4.27: Steps for workforce reduction

S. no.	Attribute category	High performing	Low performing
1	No steps undertaken	8	9
2	Contractisation of some tasks	1	1
3	Stop replacing outgoing employees	3	4
4	VRS	0	1
5	Combination	3	0

Annex 2

Cosmo Films Limited—The Decade of the Nineties—A Case Study[4]

It was indeed a matter of great satisfaction and honour for Cosmo Films Ltd. to be chosen as one among the 18 Indian companies (among the global companies with turnover less than 1 billion US dollars) recognised and rewarded by Forbes magazine in 2003. The company had reached an annual turnover of Rs 300 crores of which over Rs 106 crores came from exports. This continued vibrancy clearly demonstrates how the company

[4] Case authors: SC Rajsekhar and Chitra Subramaniam.

not only managed but thrived during the troublesome decade of the Nineties.

Background

In October 1996, Ashok Jaipuria, Chairman & Managing Director, Cosmo Films Ltd., (CFL) was sitting in his office in New Delhi waiting for Sushil Kumar Mittal, Head of the newly constituted Strategic Planning Group (SPG). SK Mittal had joined CFL in March 1996 and had just returned from a benchmarking survey of the US and Europe. The survey was undertaken as a part of the strategic focus of CFL to increase its exports. In the words of SK Mittal, 'It was a conscious decision for us to compete with the best and not with Third World countries.'

Indeed, faced with a situation of over-supplies, shrinking margins and cutthroat competition in the domestic market, SK Mittal had pushed for a strategy of competing in the most quality conscious and demanding of markets for BOPP. The idea was, 'If you can compete with the world's best then, we would be ready for any kind of competition in the domestic market'.

However, Jaipuria had something else on his mind. He was worried about what he observed during his recent visit to the company's plants at Aurangabad. The plants were making cash losses, credit recovery was poor, customers' cheques were bouncing and salesmen were dumping the product to achieve targets. He asked SK Mittal to investigate. Here was a company gearing itself to make bold forays into exports and was unexpectedly faced with a situation of financial weakening. He wondered what went wrong.

Cosmo Films Ltd.: The Beginning

Armed with a Degree in Associate of Arts & Diploma in Marketing Sciences from the US, Ashok Jaipuria, son of Late Sitaram Jaipuria of the famed Swadeshi Polytex, branched out to set up Cosmo Films Ltd., in October 1976. The decision to venture into BOPP was fuelled by a vision that packaging was a growing sector and afforded long-term business prospects. CFL is regarded as a pioneer in the BOPP industry in the country. Other group companies include Cosmo Ferrites and Cosmo Plantgene.

The turnover of CFL rose from Rs 72 lakhs in 1981 (its first year of operations) to Rs 118 crores in 2000–01. Of this turnover exports accounted for 40 per cent. The PAT for 2000–01 was Rs 11.09 crores, a whopping 236 per cent increase over the previous year, 1999–2000. The focus of the company as stated in its mission statement is very clear—'Development and growth in oriented films will be our focus'.

Cosmo Films Ltd.: The Decade of the Nineties

The performance of CFL during the decade of the Nineties may be categorised into two phases, 1990–96 and Post–1996.

Phase 1: 1990–96

The end of the decade of the Eighties saw CFL with an equity base of Rs 2.45 crores and a production capacity of 3300 TPA with two plants, one each at Chikalthana and Waluj in Aurangabad. A pioneer in the field of BOPP in India, it had a good image among its peers as a well managed company. An employee-friendly approach had fostered a strong bond with its workforce.

With the advent of liberalisation and globalisation, things began to change for CFL. The opportunity presented by a zooming demand was seized with both hands. Plans to expand capacities were drawn up and equity increased from Rs 2.39 crores in 1989–90 to Rs 7.49 crores in 1995–96. Both long-term debt and equity were used to finance the expansion.

Sales increased from Rs 31.82 crores in 1990–91 to Rs 76.39 crores in 1995–96. PAT (NNRT) also increased from (–) Rs 0.42 crores to Rs 11.49 crores during the same period. Long-term debt-equity ratio decreased from 3.86 to 0.64, mainly due to increase in equity.

On the R&D front, the company developed a new product, named CMP-III that had the feel of a paper but was made of BOPP. It applied for a patent for the same. The R&D facility, Silvassa Unit and Line III at Waluj began operations taking the capacity to 11,800 TPA. The company became the first in the industry to receive ISO 9002. Line I received ISO 9001.

Until the end of this period, the company was managed directly by Ashok Jaipuria. All functions except production were based in Delhi. The plant was managed by the vice-president based in Aurangabad. Production was planned based on the demand projected by marketing personnel from the various regions.

This phase was characterised by an upbeat sentiment that demand would continue to grow at over 25 per cent and that the product would be in short supply. Thus a planning system that was based on demand projections worked well, even if the projections were inaccurate. The same sentiment extended to implementing Line III. The company felt that it could fabricate major parts of the machinery itself, instead of purchasing from its regular overseas suppliers. As Ranbir Mukherjee, President CFL, puts it,' Cosmo as an organisation had become arrogant and haughty. So much so that it even thought of making its own lines!' The company was in a seller's market and felt supremely confident of itself.

Phase 2: Post–1996
By the end of 1995–96, Jaipuria felt the need to professionalise the company to take advantage of the growing opportunities that liberalisation was offering and opted out of day to day management. He created a Strategic Planning Group to chart out a strategic plan for the entire group. He invited SK Mittal, a Chartered Accountant working with Samtel to head it. SK Mittal says, 'It was the man I chose, not the company. Our wavelengths matched.'

This phase saw the reversal of fortunes for CFL. A booming market suddenly went bust. Over-capacities meant thinner margins, and a change in market from seller's to buyer's. From a PAT (NNRT) of Rs 11.49 crores in 1996, the company plummeted to just Rs 6.26 crores in the very next year.

As R. Mukherjee says, 'The company was very successful during the period 1992–96. But for all the wrong reasons. The first jolt to us came not from (cheaper imports) liberalisation, but because of domestic competition. We had to change our mindset to do business in the new environment.'

This was when Jaipuria had asked to SK Mittal to investigate the situation that CFL faced. He returned from Aurangabad with a report that outlined the reasons:

- Poor capacity utilisation
- Poor credit recovery

- Dumping of product to achieve sales targets
- High interest burden
- Long-term loans were taken at very high interest rates of 17–19 per cent when the current rates were about 12–15 per cent
- High rejection rates in both Lines II & III
- Most importantly, low employee morale

In response Jaipuria asked SK Mittal to take charge of the plants at Aurangabad as President of CFL. Simultaneously, they began looking for a person to revamp production facilities and quality in order to meet the stringent needs of catering to the export markets. Through some contacts in Philips India, Pune, Jaipuria identified Ranbir Mukherjee as a possible candidate.

Initially, he agreed to come one day every month to study the problem at CFL, Aurangabad. R. Mukherjee recalls,' I had just then taken VRS from Philips and wanted to see what I was getting myself into. Soon I found myself getting very interested and involved. Of course as an outsider, I could ask a lot of questions on why things were being done the way they were. It did help me later on when I took charge in September 1997.'

As R. Mukherjee says, 'The company was very successful during the period 1992–96. But for all the wrong reasons. The first jolt to us came not from (cheaper imports) liberalisation, but because of domestic competition. We had to change our mindset to do business in the new environment.'

On an analysis Jaipuria and SK Mittal found that the company's financial woes were the most pressing of the problems. They decided to tackle it at once, since it had a direct bearing on the bottom-line of the company.

Finance

Cosmo had been a high debt company throughout the late Eighties and the early Nineties. The high dependence on debt continued till 1992–93 with debt equity ratio hovering above 3. Financing through equity emerged in 1993–94, when zero interest convertible debentures were issued. Increase in equity resulted in the lowering of the debt to equity ratio to 1.41. A further issue of equity shares in the subsequent year 1994–95 brought down the ratio to 0.43, 1995–96, saw a further increase in long-term borrowings to meet the expansion programme, taking the ratio to 0.64. In 1997–98, the ratio had again risen to 0.87, the rise due to increase in long-term borrowings due to obligations arising out the FCD issue.

SK Mittal found that the company was groaning under the burden of costly debts and high interest was eating into profits. The problem of interest burden on the profitability of the company can be seen when comparing PBDIT/sales and PBDT/sales.

Table 4.28: Cosmo Film Ltd. Finance: PBDIT/Sales and PBDT/Sales

Year	PBDIT/sales (%)	PBDT/sales (%)
1995–96	22.11	18.54
1996–97	19.13	11.46
1997–98	10.49	–0.67
1998–99	12.88	3.54
1999–2000	15.71	8.67

Source: PROWESS—Centre for monitoring Indian Economy Pvt. Ltd. Mumbai.

Costly debt was retired prematurely. It was swapped for lower interest rate redeemable preference shares. Long-term borrowings came down to Rs 30.45 crores in 1999–2000 from a high of Rs 49.27 crores, the previous year. Plans are to redeem the preference shares in the coming months. Increase in profitability also helped generate internal accruals.

By the year 2000–01, CFL paid off nearly all it costly debts and balance portion of the 15 per cent redeemable non-convertible debentures. Investments for plant expansion (Line IV) has been funded through internal accruals to the tune of Rs 25 crores and borrowings from IDBI for Rs 22 crores.

A change in policy from ' Produce and then sell' to 'Produce to confirmed orders' meant faster turnover of inventories and better receivables management. As on March 2001 the total debtors was Rs 19.53 crores as against Rs 25.40 crores in the previous year. Inventories as a percentage of sales fell from 11 per cent to 10 per cent.

Speaking of the changes brought about to remedy the financial situation, SK Mittal says, 'The company used its financial resources in a better way. We are enjoying suppliers' credit. Implementation of Avalon along with the policy of producing only against confirmed orders has helped in better inventory management. Finished goods inventory has come down from 36 days to just 2 days.'

This has had an impact on the working capital cycle too. The holding period (no. of days) has come down from a high of 86 days in 1995–96 to 58 in 1999–2000. The net working capital cycle also moved downwards from 131 days to 101 days during the same period. Impact on the working capital requirement has been substantial. From a high of Rs 27.10 crores in 1998–99 it has reduced to Rs 22.46 crores in 1999–2000.

Soon after R. Mukherjee's joining, he and SK Mittal decided to tackle the other problems of the company.

Organisation

Until the end of 1995–96, CFL was a promoter driven and managed organisation. Good HR practices such as periodic training for the employees, introduction of TQM, etc. were in vogue. However, decision-making was centralised at Delhi. All functions except production were being handled from the corporate office. Commenting on this R. Mukherjee says, 'This separation of vital functions such as marketing from manufacturing was not working well. There was no understanding between the two. The whole organisation suffered from this attitude of Marketing vs Manufacturing. The first decision I took was to integrate the two and move them to the plant at Aurangabad.'

Soon other departments also followed; accounts, HR, exports and commercial. Only corporate affairs and investor relations are now managed from Delhi. R&D facility at Silvassa was wound-up and moved to Aurangabad. This move saved the organisation substantially in terms of time spent in communication and coordination. Land that was acquired at Nashik for future expansion was sold off in view of the decision to consolidate all production at Aurangabad.

Speaking of the situation when he took over R. Mukherjee recalls, 'The climate in the organisation also changed. People were not taking initiative for fear of being punished for failures. Interpersonal relationships were very poor among the employees and also with customers. The company lacked a culture of mutual interaction and participation. It simply was not functioning as a cohesive business organisation.

'Yet the same company was making profits just a year back. Indeed, they were successful, but for all the wrong reasons. What the company lacked was good management. The first step we felt was to get buy-in from all that it was worth running this company and running it well, based on basic values of honesty, transparency and responsiveness.'

SK Mittal and R. Mukherjee spent a lot of time in interacting with employees at various levels to understand their problems, apprehensions and the job they were entrusted with. They decided to focus on successes rather than failures. 'We wanted to replace the climate of fear of failure to one based on building on successes. In our analysis of the problems we were not interested in the person committing mistakes, but in identifying the causes and tackling them', says R. Mukherjee. The approach slowly began paying dividends. The climate in the organisation changed. With the integration of marketing and manufacturing, the schism that permeated the company also vanished. There was better interaction among the staff and this led to improvement in morale.

The next step attempted by the company was business process reengineering (BPR). R. Mukherjee explains, 'Using the Hay's System, we evaluated every job in the company. Based on the jobs identified, we prepared a professional JD (job description) for all posts upto the level of Deputy Manager with no reference to the existing person. Then we matched the job requirements with the personnel. Right people for the right job.'

This process and appraisal system helped the company reduce its workforce by 30 per cent. Today, the corporate office functions with just 10 persons and the entire plant and all other functions are manned by just 350 persons at Aurangabad. Sales per employee has increased from 0.6 MT in 1997–98 to 1.56 MT in 1999–2000.

Once the climate was good in the organisation, they introduced an 'Open Appraisal System'. Rakhunde, Manager, HR says, 'It was important that the climate was good before all these changes were made. Otherwise, they may not have given the desired results.'

To build an organisation to compete in the changed situation, the need was for a quick and responsive workforce. Job rotations were introduced to increase cross-functional ability. SK Mittal says, ' Mukherjee and I experiment a lot with employees. We rotate people so that they may learn new things and realise their potential better. This ensures that the mindset not to change, also changes! Today nearly 70 per cent of the people in export marketing are from R&D.'

Employees are kept up to date with training programmes and lectures. SK Mittal (Bullet-proof Manager) and R. Mukherjee (Managers to Leaders) themselves conduct some of the trainings. An evidence of commitment by the top management to trainings. Monthly review meetings and project reviews meetings are also places where information is exchanged in a free manner.

The company has an in-house newsletter called Cosmic. Cosmic forms the plank for communications with the staff. It also encourages the creative aspiration of employees. Happenings, details of training programmes held, visits by buyers, researchers are all shared. Cosmo Today is a letter to the shareholders from the Chairman's desk. Technical bulletins are regularly mailed to customers and Quarterly Audited Financial Results are published for investors as a part of Good Corporate Governance.

Speaking about the vibrancy now evident in the organisation, SK Mittal says with justifiable pride, 'For an organisation the mindset for winning should be 'keep on learning—keep on trying'. The environment is such that one needs to be flexible. To succeed risk taking is essential. However, no person has been fired for committing a mistake, as long as the efforts were genuine.'

Atul Mittal, Company Secretary says, ' The commitment to openness in the organisation is genuine from the top management. In fact, if we are convinced that an issue has to be handled in a particular way, then we simply put it up to the management. The issue is analysed and if we can convince the others about the effectiveness of such a step, it is accepted and a go ahead is given. The current plant expansion is because everyone felt the need to expand capacity, it was not a decision taken by the management one fine morning.'

SK Mittal is a man with immense and unshakable faith in HR and people. 'If people are attuned anything can be achieved. Our human resource talent is less than none in the world. What can be achieved in IT can be achieved anywhere.'

The thrust on HR is yielding rich dividends. No increase in employees is envisaged after commissioning of Line IV/Line V. The plan is to run it with the existing workforce. 'People have tremendous potential which if tapped effectively can produce best results', says SK Mittal. 'An organisation that is quick, responsive and transparent has been created. Now we aim to break into the world's top 10 BOPP company's in the next 2 years time.'

Production

During the decade of the Nineties, CFL increased its capacity to 14000 TPA by adding a new line (Line III) of 9000 TPA. Recalling the state of the plant R. Mukherjee says, ' Productivity was low and wastages were high. About Rs 3.5 crores worth of goods came back every year from the customer as rejections. Line III was a mess. It was based on a design provided by our French suppliers but made by Cosmo itself! It broke down frequently and first time rejections were very high—about 11.05 per cent of production.'

The first step undertaken was revamp of Line III. Incompatible parts and assemblies were identified and replaced by originals sourced from the French supplier. Today, R. Mukherjee says with pride, 'Line III contributes Rs 50,000 every hour and it has a uptime of 7200 hours! In fact, we now record uptime and not downtime.'

During his visits before he joined CFL, R. Mukherjee had observed that the lines were overstaffed. An example is the slitting section. Earlier, there were 20 secondary slitters each operated by 2 persons. The jumbo rolls coming off the line were further cut into custom sizes on these secondary slitters. The primary slitters on the line were hardly used. A study of the operations was made and after trial and errors, the primary slitters were used for most of the slitting and only the very final cut was sent to the secondary slitters. This helped reduce the no. of slitting machines from 20 to just 8. In addition, R. Mukherjee also found that 2 operators were not needed and one person could handle the rolls, thread the slitter and observe the operations. Thus staff was reduced in this section from 40 to just 8. The reduction in the no. of slitters helped release space for handling the finished goods and the lines became more streamlined.

Another major change was the winding up of the Quality Inspection department. As R. Mukherjee says, ' There were 20 Quality Inspectors and the market returns were about Rs 3.5 crores. Now we have no Quality Inspectors and market returns is less than Rs 10 lakhs per year. The best way to ensure good quality consistently is to make sure the manufacturing process is perfect.' In fact, today, the reasons for rejection are marked on the market returned goods and displayed on the shop floor so that the operators may receive the feedback.

Similarly, Line I, the oldest line at Chiklathana was also revamped. Workforce was reduced from 128 to just 42 to run the line. Today, it is running at more than 100 per cent capacity.

However, the major change was in the policy of production. From a system of 'produce and sell' the company moved to 'Produce only against confirmed orders'. This needed a fast and responsive production system. After much deliberations the company chose to go in for an ERP system from TCS called Avalon.

Speaking about the timing of ERP implementation, R. Mukherjee says, 'If we had decided to go for an ERP in 1995 itself we would still have been discussing on how to implement. Since we had created an open climate in the organisation and had already implemented our own BPR, it was easy to customise Avalon to suit our needs.'

Today, the company is aggressively implementing Line IV and expects it to be on stream by end of September, 2001. As SK Mittal says, ' We have today, a production system that can deliver products from 10 microns to 70 microns of world class quality. We are able to compete in low volume, high-value added segments due to our flexible manufacturing system and high skill levels of our operators.'

Marketing and R&D

The sales of the company grew steadily in the decade of Nineties. From Rs 21.9 crores (gross sales) in 1989–90, it has risen to Rs 112.99 crores in 1999–2000. For the year 2000–01, the gross sales was Rs 130.24 crores and net sales Rs 118 crores. The company's sales have grown at an approximate 20 per cent except for the year 1992–93 when it was only 1.64 per cent and in 1997–98 when it registered a negative growth rate, i.e., fell by 15.46 per cent.

The company began with plain films for lamination and pressure sensitive tapes. Soon it realised the need to move into value-added segments such as heat-sealable films, and variants such as metallised, opaque and pearlised. Currently, the company caters to both the export and the domestic markets.

Domestic Markets

Upto 1995–96, domestic markets accounted for more than 90 per cent of total sales. The main customers were cigarette manufacturers, FMCG companies and packaged food companies.

However, over-capacity in the industry and sluggish domestic demand forced the company to take a re-look at their product mix.

As SK Mittal says, 'We decided to exit from areas where the realisations were very low and the market was unorganised. For example, we moved out of the pressure sensitive tapes segment, because margins were low and payment terms not very good. Earlier we used to sell about 150 MT a year. Now we are content with just 20–30 MT. We are maintaining a token presence to keep a watch on this market segment.'

A major change was the shift to 'production only against confirmed orders'. SK Mittal says, 'Earlier, we produced based on the forecast provided by the sales personnel. If it were 90 per cent accurate, we could have continued, but it was less than 30–40 per cent. So we decided to change the system. Initially, it was tough for both salesmen and customers to adjust to the system. But we stuck to our policy and soon everyone fell in line.

'Another change was in pricing. We decided to do away with discounts. This was leading to arbitrary and whimsical decisions. Instead we introduced a system of fixing prices valid for month. Since raw material prices are also fixed on a monthly basis, this fitted in nicely.'

The strategy for the domestic market has been to move away from crowded and unorganised market segments and instead focus on creating value addition for the customer. The company has been aided in this regard by the excellent efforts of its R&D division.

The company received ISO 9002 in December 1994 and the coveted ISO 9001 in 1996 for its plants at Chikalthana and Waluj.

CFL became the first BOPP company in the country to receive certification covering design, development and manufacturing. Emphasis on R&D in the company dates back to the late Eighties. CMPIII (Synthetic Paper) was first developed then.

Another contribution from the R&D department towards creating customised and value-added product is the development of packaging for Hindustan Lever Ltd.,'s Lifebuoy soap. With a predominant rural consumption, transporting it to far off areas meant a weight loss of 5–6 per cent due to evaporation of moisture content, in addition to the problems during monsoons. Cosmo came up with an innovative BOPP over-wrap. The BOPP film was placed over the traditional paper pack. This gave higher visibility to the company's logo and a glossy and protective outer-cover that would protect it during monsoons and prevent weight loss.

Today CFL spends about 1 per cent of its sales on R&D. Indeed, this department has made a substantial contribution to the bottom-line of the company. With the company getting a patent for its synthetic paper and about 4–5 products on the verge of getting patented, the future looks secure on this front.

Exports

Exports have been the driving force for the quick turnaround by the company from the situation it found itself in 1997–98. The company had some export sales during the earlier years too. However, the share of exports to the total sales of the company was minuscule. In 1989–90 it constituted just about 2.56 per cent of sales. This share further fell during the period 1990–94, whereafter it rose to 2.57 per cent & 3.95 per cent in the years 1994–95 and 1995–96.

In response to the slowdown in the latter half of 1996–97, increase in domestic capacity and a sagging bottom-line, Cosmo made a conscious decision of getting into exports as a part of its marketing strategy. As SK Mittal puts it, 'exports not for capacity utilisation but as USP to compete. Exports were a conscious decision to compete with the best and not to compete with the third world.'

Demand for BOPP in the US and Europe is high and has been growing at a healthy 6–7 per cent. However, competition is tough too, with major players in the fray. To counter tough competition and market conditions the company decided to find niche markets that yielded higher realisation at lower volumes. One such product identified and developed was very thin films for lamination. Since the film is very thin, the customer saves on tonnage and also cost. The thinking was such areas would not be lucrative for big players used to dealing in high volumes. As Mittal puts it, 'Production is complicated for such products requiring adjustments and with low volumes, it is not attractive for players with huge capacities.'

Talking of their experience with the export market, Mittal says, 'Breakthrough was very difficult. Even now it takes a lot of convincing for buyers to accept products from India.' He recounts the case of an Italian buyer identified 3.5 years ago. Initially he gave them an order of only 1 container. After a couple of orders he came to visit the plant. He was thoroughly impressed and Cosmo angled for a higher order quantity of 20–40 MT. 'He really haggled for price' and went back to Italy from where he sent an L/C for 40 MT. He finishes saying, 'Last month I went to Italy. He gave us a huge order with a blank price saying he trusted us on it.'

He adds, 'To earn this trust one has to work really hard. In the international market, there is little room for mistakes. You get only one or two chances in most cases after which you are out for ever. So for us every shipment is critical and we take it as a do or die situation. The bent of mind is towards zero defect.'

Says R. Mukherjee, 'When we decided to focus on exports as a thrust area, we started pursuing customers abroad. Soon we found that it was not enough to market. We needed to develop products for customers. We then decided that the best person to meet customers was our best technical person—the Head of R&D. He had no experience in marketing and much less in commercial areas. Initially, I supported him, soon he learnt and today, our Exports team has many R&D personnel.'

The strategy of focus on exports has paid off. Export earnings have swelled and in 2000–01 it was Rs 33.60 crores accounting for 40 per cent of total sales by volume. Cosmo has started focussing on markets other than the US for its products. It has filed for patents, which when granted would safeguard its products and markets in the days to come. Customised products also help in raising barriers to competition.

Conclusion

The decade of the Nineties was a tumultuous one for the BOPP industry in India. Forces of liberalisation brought with it tremendous opportunities for growth. During the first half of the decade the industry was in a seller's market. However, lack of entry barriers meant that new companies entered the market and capacity doubled. This led to a situation of over-supply, thinner margins and tough competition in the domestic market.

Each company in the industry tried its own ways of coping with the changed situation. Cosmo Films Ltd., against all conventional thinking, decided on a strategy of focusing on exports. The thinking was, competing with the best in the most demanding markets would help tune the company to face any challenges in the domestic markets.

The company also saw a change in management. From being a promoter-managed company it became a professionally managed one with the induction of SK Mittal as CEO and R. Mukherjee as President. Curiously, both had no experience in the industry before joining CFL. Indeed, as SK Mittal remarks, ' Managing a new industry is not very difficult. Managing its people is the key.'

Speaking of the future he says, ' Today, we have built an organisation that is flexible, transparent and quick in its response. We have decided to focus on our core competence—BOPP. We are prepared to face any challenges from anyone, because we are well-tuned to respond to change quickly. Today we are focused on exports. Tomorrow if the domestic market picks-up we are ready for it. The key to this flexibility is managing people, changing their mindset.' Indeed, that is SK Mittal and CFL's secret formula for success.

Annex 2.1

Time-Line of Events

Cosmo Films Ltd. was set up in 1976. In 1980 Cosmo Films secured loans for Rs 3 crores from a consortium of financial institutions (ICICI, IDBI & IFCI). It also came out with its IPO of 9 lakh shares at par. Of which 4,41,000 shares were offered to the public and the balance of 4,59,000 shares were issued to the promoters. The company was listed as a public limited company in 1980–81.

In 1981, it was given a licence for packaging for the State of Maharashtra, this sowed the seeds for its innings with BOPP films.

It began its operations in 1981 with a plant capacity of 800 TPA at Chikalthana in Aurangabad. In 1988 the company also came out with its rights cum public issue at Rs 40 per share (Rs 10 face value and Rs 30 premium). The company went in for a further expansion of 4000 TPA around 1989. An issue of Non Convertible Debenture (NCD) and rights cum public issue met the funding for this expansion and other needs. During the same period another 14 per cent NCD was made for Rs 1 crore. A 15 per cent NCD issue was made for Rs 50,00,000.

1990–91: The company went in for its share of FCNR as with the devaluation of rupee, foreign loans became popular.

1991–92: A specialised BOPP film brand name CMP–111 was developed by CFL. This felt like paper and had all the advantage of it. It also applied for patents for the same. A secured convertible debenture issue on a rights basis at an aggregate face value of Rs 18.22 crores was also planned.

1992–93: The company came out with a zero interest secured fully convertible debenture issue in January 93 of 15,18,425 debentures @ Rs 120 per debenture. Part A—to be converted into 2 equity shares at par (Rs 10/-) after 6 months. Part B—also to be converted into equity shares in March 97, with a put option.

1993–94: It converted Part I of debenture into 30,36,850 equity shares. Share capital of the company increased from Rs 2.45 crores to Rs 5.49 crores. It planned to expand capacity by Line III at Waluj. It also issued Commercial Paper of Rs 5 crores for working capital requirements for which it was given the highest rating P1+ by Crisil.

1994–95: Ten lakh equity shares were issued to the promoters and another 10 lakh equity shares to Foreign Financial Institutions and Indian Mutual Funds. This increased the equity share capital from Rs 5.49 crores to 7.49 crores. It also started leasing and international trading operations. The company was given ISO 9002 certification in December 1994. Thus making it the first Indian BOPP company to get such a certification. It began operations at Silvassa. It also began the implementation of Line III at Waluj. The capacity addition was expected to be 7000 TPA. The financing of this expansion was through term loans and equity issue. Cosmo Fininvest Pvt. Ltd. became a subsidiary of the company.

1995–96: CFL began commercial production at Silvassa. The total capacity increased to 12,700 TPA. It commenced the commercial production of Line III at Waluj. It also received an ISO 9001 certification. A Strategic Planning Group was created and Sushil K Mittal joined as President. CFL envisaged a further capacity expansion of 15,000 TPA and planned to set up a factory of international standards.

1996–97: During this year Part B of FCD were converted. 73 per cent of holders opted for put and non-conversion option. These holders were paid interest for the entire tenure of the debenture from its date of allotment (January 1993). 10,32.500 debentures were to be redeemed in 3 instalments in 6th, 7th and 8th year from the date of allotment. Balance debenture holders were alloted shares at a premium of Rs 44 per share. The total number of shares alloted was 7,51,204. The share capital of the company increased from Rs 7.49 crores to Rs 8.24 crores and has remained the same till 2000–2001. It started a process of focussing only on BOPP. All allied activities like trading were discontinued. Line III was totally revamped and capacity was marginally raised to 14,000 TPA. The company made plans to set up a 17000 TPA plant at Nasik. A wholly owned subsidiary Cosmo International Limited was set up in Mauritius to take care of exports to South Africa. 19 per cent Secured Redeemable non-convertible debentures worth Rs 2.5 crores were privately placed with LIC Mutual Fund.

1997– 98: SK Mittal was made the President of CFL. It moved out of areas, markets which were not found competitive and focussed only on BOPP. The implementation of ERP was begun. The capacity expansion at Waluj was completed. The R&D of products was emphasised and 4 new product/applications were developed. The organisation was restructured and revamped. The company made an operating cash loss of Rs 42 crores and a net loss of Rs 1.44 crores. 19 per cent Secured Redeemable non-convertible debentures were issued for Rs 5 crores, taking the amount to Rs 7.5 crores.

1998–99: SK Mittal was made the Executive Director in-charge of the entire running of Cosmo Films Ltd. He can be called the architect of its turnaround and evolution as a well managed, transparent, professional company. The company made an operating cash profit of Rs 3.9 crores and a net loss of Rs 2.34 crores. It went in for financial restructuring and its term loans were restructured. A part of the term loans not exceeding Rs 800 lakhs were converted into 13 per cent cumulative preference shares. The turnaround strategy focussed on exports, cost cutting exercise, tightening operations and on R&D, for development of newer products. The company's focus was BOPP. The operation of its works at Silvassa was shut down.

1999–2000: As a result of these tough measures, the company achieved turnaround. It made a net profit after tax of Rs 3.33 crores. There was further thrust on exports, cost cutting and operational efficiency. It won the Best BOPP exporter award and filed for 4 more patents. The implementation of ERP package was completed. A further capacity expansion by way of a new 9000 TPA plant was proposed at the existing location—Waluj. The 19 per cent secured redeemable NCD were prepaid. It also issued 8 lakhs 13 per cent cumulative redeemable preference shares of Rs 100 each to be redeemed on the expiry of 4th, 5th and 6th year from the date of allotment.

2000–01: The company achieved a net profit of Rs 11.09 crores. The combination of cost cutting exercise, thrust on export market and in niches where realisations were high and operational efficiency helped achieve this. It filed for 2 more patents and there was increased thrust on R&D. It received patent for Synthetic Paper, the first BOPP manufacturer in India to do so. The Waluj plant expansion was completed. Cosmo International Limited at Mauritius was wound up. Cosmo International (US) Inc., which was set up in 1998 to sell packing material, became a direct subsidiary of Cosmo Films Ltd. It sold off all unrelated investments—NPAs, real estate. The investments in Cosmo Ferrites and Cosmo Plantgene, however remained. The land that was bought at Nasik was also sold. The 15 per cent NCD were redeemed fully. The plant at Waluj is being funded by internal accruals and term loans from IDBI.

2001: The plant at Waluj Line IV/Line V to be operational in September. Costly debt retired.

Annex 2.2

Figure 4.1: Organogram

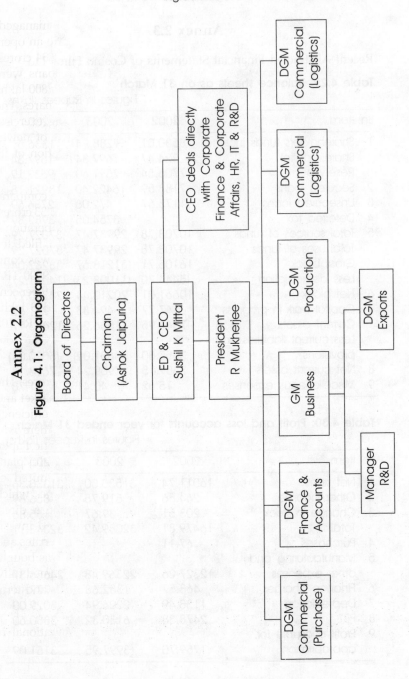

Annex 2.3

Recent Abstracted Financial Statements of Cosmo Films Ltd.

Table 4.29: Balance sheets as on 31 March

Figures in Rupees (lakhs)

Sn.	Item	2002	2003	2004
1	Shareholders funds includes	8530.01	9288.94	11336.5
	Share capital	824.47	1697.34	1697.34
	Reserves	7705.54	7591.60	9639.19
2	Secured loans	7183.59	16422.40	18921.18
3	Unsecured loans	1173.67	472.08	2786.69
4	Deferred tax		3754.05	3982.89
5	Total sources of funds	10708.78	29937.47	37027.29
	Total uses of funds	10708.78	29937.47	37027.29
	Gross block	16105.71	31218.67	38282.04
	Less depreciation	(5444.70)	(11008.23)	(14031.27)
6	Net block	10661.01	20210.44	24250.77
7	Capital work in progress	47.77	494.33	211.62
	Current assets	7344.95	11566.26	12623.17
	Less current liabilities and provisions	3855.80	(3657.02)	(5010.04)
8	Net current assets	3489.15	7909.24	7613.13
9	Miscellaneous expenses	15.62	40.41	31.78

Table 4.30: Profit and loss accounts for year ended 31 March

Figures in Rupees (lakhs)

Sn.	Item	2002	2003	2004
1	Net sales	16011.74	31530.00	31330.36
2	Other income	264.56	519.75	856.89
3	Change in stock	203.51	39.67	155.86
	Total	16479.81	32089.42	32343.11
4	Purchases	67.11	–	–
5	Manufacturing and other expenses	12327.26	22369.48	24656.37
6	Finance charges	468.57	1382.68	777.14
7	Depreciation	1138.49	2206.94	3029.00
8	PBT	2478.38	6130.32	3880.60
9	Profit available for appropriation	1759.70	3997.95	3151.09

Table 4.31: Profit and loss account (Rs in crore) non-annualised

	Mar 1990	Mar 1991	Mar 1992	Mar 1993	Mar 1994	Mar 1995	Mar 1996	Mar 1997	Mar 1998	Mar 1999	Mar 2000
Gross sales	21.90	31.82	39.55	40.20	52.01	61.55	76.39	94.25	79.68	101.35	112.99
Net sales	17.58	25.61	31.34	31.63	40.00	47.31	61.13	76.14	66.34	85.30	97.60
VOP	18.32	26.11	31.00	31.39	39.09	47.41	62.59	78.57	65.50	84.03	96.82
Other income	0.34	0.33	0.39	0.82	0.89	2.26	3.27	2.47	1.97	1.24	1.16
Cost of production	14.56	19.79	22.84	23.01	26.67	32.03	44.86	59.15	53.84	66.53	74.77
Selling cost	0.28	0.50	0.66	0.89	1.12	1.45	1.86	2.35	3.22	4.76	5.34
PBDIT (NNRT)	4.18	6.16	8.24	8.48	10.72	14.33	16.89	18.03	8.36	13.05	17.75
PBDT (NNRT)	0.65	1.81	3.09	3.47	8.24	12.15	14.61	10.80	(0.53)	3.59	9.80
PBT (NNRT)	(1.57)	(0.42)	0.82	1.03	6.53	10.47	11.50	6.29	(5.53)	(2.21)	3.35
PAT (NNRT)	(1.57)	(0.42)	0.82	1.03	6.52	10.31	11.49	6.26	(5.56)	(2.23)	3.86

Source: PROWESS—Centre for monitoring Indian Economy Pvt. Ltd. Mumbai.

Balance sheet (Rs in crore)

	Mar 1990	Mar 1991	Mar 1992	Mar 1993	Mar 1994	Mar 1995	Mar 1996	Mar 1997	Mar 1998	Mar 1999	Mar 2000
Gross fixed assets (net of reval & WIP)	30.05	31.02	32.70	36.07	36.59	42.57	82.99	95.78	110.33	112.66	109.98
Current assets	11.46	16.21	18.77	20.86	23.42	35.36	47.13	45.69	47.04	50.30	52.36
Net worth	6.24	6.11	7.11	7.75	16.53	47.24	57.01	61.54	59.25	56.95	66.44
Equity capital	2.39	2.39	2.39	2.46	5.49	7.49	7.49	8.24	8.24	8.24	8.24
Long-term borrowings	22.19	23.60	23.29	27.67	23.16	20.12	36.50	38.74	51.29	49.27	30.45
Capital employed	28.43	29.71	30.40	35.42	39.69	67.36	93.51	100.28	110.54	106.22	96.89
Current liabilities & provisions	7.89	10.24	11.24	10.15	10.08	10.76	27.68	27.88	30.04	34.03	37.45
Total assets/liabilities	36.30	39.93	41.61	45.52	49.68	77.58	120.70	127.79	140.39	139.84	133.76

Source: PROWESS—Centre for monitoring Indian Economy Pvt. Ltd. Mumbai.

Annex 2.4

Table 4.32: Comparison of key parameters showing turnaround of CFL

S. no.	Particular	1997–98	1998–99	1999–2000
1.	Sales-exports in MT	1797	1941	2532
2.	Sales-domestic in MT	4505	5859	5816
3.	Sales/person in MT	0.60	0.90	1.56
4.	Finished goods inventory in Rs lakhs	398.28	283.70	154.28
5.	Work in progress in Rs lakhs	31.06	18.78	70.25
6.	Date of accounts finalisation	25 June 1998	31 May 1999	1 May 2000
7.	Communication costs in Rs lakhs	89.39	84.95	65.13
8.	% sales returns of despatch	2.89	1.73	0.51
9.	I hand rejection for Line II as % of production	11.37	3.71	3.43
10.	I hand rejection for Line III as % of production	11.05	3.14	2.64
11.	Average monthly sales in MT	525	650	724

Source: Company Records.

Annex 2.5

What is BOPP?

BOPP, bi-axially oriented poly-propylene, is used extensively in packaging and lamination. It has replaced cellophane and aluminium foil due to its versatility and relative inexpensiveness. Today, it is used in industries such as cigarettes, processed foods, confectioneries, maps, visiting cards, magazine laminations, toiletries, etc.

BOPP films are produced by either the Stenter or the Bubble Process. The Stenter process is more popular. Poly-propylene, homopolymer and certain additives (depending on the properties desired in the final product) are heated and extruded as a flat film onto chilled rolls. The first stretching is in the direction of the film called MDO (machine direction orientation) and then in the traverse direction called TDO (traverse direction orientation). This processing increases the tensile strength of the film, its flexibility, shrinkability etc.

The main features of BOPP films for packaging are:

- High clarity, high strength, excellent moisture barrier. Useful for products that are sensitive to water.
- Can be produced with single side or both sides heat-sealable surface. Speeds up packaging process by eliminating the need for applying adhesives, etc.
- Several surface finishes are possible—matt or bright shiny, pearlised, opaque in different colours, metallised with matt or bright shiny finish. Is transparent and is glossy.
- Highest yield when compared with other packaging films.
- High tensile strength and low elongation at break. This quality comes handy in products like pressure sensitive tapes.
- High tear initiation. But once it breaks, it is easier to tear. So if the pack has perforation, it can be easily torn by the consumer.
- Good barriers to flavours and aroma.
- It has high chemical resistance to oils, hence suitable for direct food contact.
- Does not promote bacterial growth.

Since BOPP combines each of these qualities with economy, it is an excellent choice to develop a packaging that offers economy, utility and shelf appeal. The main consumers are FMCG manufacturers, cigarette companies, food products manufacturers and converting industry.

There are three basic variants in BOPP, namely, Pressure Sensitive Tapes, Heat Sealable Tapes and Synthetic Paper. Pressure Sensitive Tapes could be for Print Lamination, Thermolamination or for Release Applications. Heat Sealable films are used for Snack Food Packaging and as Overwrap in textiles, blades, cigarettes and in wraparound labels. Synthetic Paper is used for visiting cards, maps, posters and calendars. In each of these variants, the finish could be glossy, opaque, pearlised, metallised, etc. The choice of films as per SK Mittal is, 'basically based on marketability and shelf-life'.

BOPP—International Scenario

OPP (Oriented Poly-propylene) is a preferred choice for packaging and lamination in the international markets. Specifically it registered high growth in the Seventies and Eighties before settling down to growth rates of 6–7 per cent in the Nineties. The market is characterised by huge investments and large volumes. Demand in the world market is pegged at 2.5–3 million tonnes per annum. Manufacturers are present in almost all countries and include, US, Italy, UK, Germany, Korea, China, Italy, Japan, Indonesia, Australia. World production units are characterised by huge capacities. As SK Mittal says, 'The smallest among the world's top 10 BOPP units have capacities in excess of 50,000 TPA'.

BOPP—Indian Scenario During the Nineties

Till the Nineties, BOPP industry in India was characterised by small capacities and very few players such as, Gujarat Propak, Max, CFL, etc. However, with the advent of liberalisation and globalisation, the prospects for the BOPP industry changed. The scenario of the Indian BOPP industry during the Nineties can be categorised into two phases: 1992–96 and Post–1996.

Phase 1: 1992–96

Capacity in the BOPP film industry was a tiny 800 TPA in early 1982. This then rose to around 2,400 TPA in 1985–86 and to 5300 TPA in the late Eighties. This figure rose to 17,000 TPA in 1991–92.

With the advent of liberalisation and globalisation, indications and anticipation were strong that the packaging industry would boom. As a result, BOPP (whose advantages far outweigh other alternatives in flexible packaging) was expected to grow at approximately 25 per cent per annum.

Further impetus was provided by the government in the form of duty cuts on imports, when custom duty on imports of raw material was reduced to 65 per cent. Adding to the optimistic predictions was increase in international demand for BOPP. Demand in the markets of US and Europe was growing at 8–10 per cent. There was significant scope for exports. The environment in the domestic sector also proved conducive. There were further cuts in import duty with custom duty on poly-propylene reduced to 50 per cent. The domestic market was expected to maintain the growth rate of 25 per cent.

Small production capacities in the industry meant that existing players were suddenly in a seller's market. Demand exceeded supply. With MNCs entering the Indian market for FMCGs and Consumer Durables in a big way, demand for packaging was rising. The growth rate of 25 per cent per annum continued and there were hopes that it would be sustained.

The demand-supply gap attracted new investments in capacities from both existing and new players. CFL increased its capacity by 8500 TPA. Flex Industries which was until then a converter went in for backward integration and put up a 15,000 TPA BOPP plant and a 24,000 TPA PET plant. Given the easy access to funds from financial institutions in the country, most of these investments came in the form of debt.

Phase 2: Post–1996

The period 1996–98 saw capacities doubling. The total capacity increased to 50,000 TPA. However, demand did not grow as expected. Internationally prices fell and the increased capacity started feeling more like a burden than an asset. From the second half of 1996–97, slow down and reversal set in. Increase in capacity of polyester films, sluggish markets, South East Asia melt down all made matters worse. Over capacity problems started plaguing the industry. Supply far exceeded demand. Industry on an average was operating at 50 per cent capacity.

Though industry conditions were a cause for the down trend, most veterans of the trade believe, companies were not prepared to respond to the changed environment. Complacency and 'taking it for granted' attitude also contributed in equal measure to the downward trend. As SK Mittal, CEO Cosmo Films says, 'What changed was the way business was done. What was needed was a different mindset. The industry grew up requiring different service and quality standards.'

Above all inefficiencies could not be sustained in the competitive environment. The high debt-equity ratios prevalent in the industry, brought with it heavy fixed expense in the form of interest cost. High interest cost on debt was difficult to bear in a situation of low sales and thin margins. Also the long-term debt at high rates of interests of 17–19 per cent proved disastrous when current rates on debt were about 12–15 per cent.

Thus the decade of the Nineties saw the demand for BOPP growing at a rapid pace of nearly 25 per cent per annum, profit-taking by existing players, huge investments in new capacities financed by liberal access to loans, untill margins came under severe pressure due to over-capacities and inefficiencies in management could not be camouflaged any longer.

Chapter Five

CAUSES OF LOW PERFORMANCE AND FAILURE IN INDIAN BUSINESS

This chapter is devoted to a discussion on decisions/actions of a firm that are associated with an inability to cope with changes in the environment, low performance, stagnation and sickness in the business. Clearly, these four consequences follow each other. A business is well-tuned to its environment—for the time-being—when the latter changes. Decision-making or actions in the business are not well-suited to the changed environment. The business starts showing signs of maladjustment: falling market-shares, piling up trade inventories, prolonging credits, withering or negative margins, reduced turnover, etc. This is essentially what poor performance is all about. As a result the interest costs mount, investible resources evaporate and the business is unable to take much corrective action. This leads to stagnation of the unit. That causes good staff to leave. Good suppliers desert the firm and so on till the business becomes sick and, in Indian parlance, 'knocks on BIFR doors.'

Some causes of this decline are more obvious than others. Also some causes are more directly associated with failures. I start with the actions that seem to be associated with those businesses that did not cope with changes in the environment. I shall then briefly touch upon some possible causes of stagnation. Finally I discuss the causes directly associated with business failures.

Poor Coping

Behavioural patterns that reduce the effectiveness of coping with changes in the environment usually involve complacence, inability to detect the changes in the environment, obstinacy is not seeing the changes even when they are unmistakable, inability to expedite action due to ossified work style, etc. At the end of this chapter, I present the case of a company named, here, *Dhanvantari Malam*. It had all the advantages one would want for a successful performance when the decade of the Nineties began. But the company had lost its premier position during the Nineties and had become a distant, also-ran by the time the century ended. The behavioural patterns that can be discerned from this company are:

- The management exhibited a high degree of complacence in relying on a decade-old formulation for the bulk of its sales. This meant that the company forgot to keep a tab on what was happening in the market. Even as competitors appeared and aggressively marketed competing products that were different but served the same mission, the company was slow to react.
- The management allowed critical time lapse in the field of research and development, seeking non-business returns from a business investment. What use would research papers in international journals be to a company, if it could not come up with new products despite spending good money on research?
- The management allowed its money resources to be invested in assorted and unrelated diversifications. These seemed to be driven as much by a desire to cash in on a new opportunity as to accommodate nephews and sons-in-law in the firm. And none of the new ventures ever became growing businesses in their own right. In other words, the company dabbled in several lines but did not follow upon any one.

This company certainly does not provide examples of unsavoury business behaviour. On the contrary, it is steeped in high-minded, brahminical ethos of moral values and stolid outlook. It had become complacent; its complacence appears to have simply dried up any entrepreneurial traits in the management. It did what most other business families were doing: starting a firm to try to cash in on every new opportunity that seemed to be good: lease finance, leather, granite, IT training, software development and call centres! All the while, its market-share dipped as its aggressive competitors designed more attractive product and packaging forms; and marketed them more aggressively using the newly popularising electronic media—truly an absence of focus.

Stagnation

If the external environment is changing in such a manner that it puts restrictions on the growth of the market for the products of the company, then stagnation is likely to result. This is because even when the company runs fast, it more or less manages to stay in its very same position in terms of market-share or volume of sales, etc. In some sense, at least the staff may perceive the stagnation—when the company management is unable to, or chooses not to take any steps to correct the above situation. (They do not try to expand geographically, introduce no new products, do not try to export, do not try to find new applications for the product etc.) And such perception may come about even if the company is actually growing at just 'demographic rate'. (Demographic rate of growth is the one that is determined by the growth in the population and the income changes that add more buyers in the income segment that, in turn, buys the company products. For instance, toilet soaps or toothpaste market may be growing only at a demographic rate.) Causes of stagnation in the extant business and for the existing set of people can also set in if the management chooses to ignore the existing business and focuses on some new venture, in which it chooses not to involve the existing set of people. Finally, stagnation may set in if the individual objective of the man at the helm of affairs changes, but still does not wish to let go of the control on the business. For instance, he may want to promote non-conventional energy as a social cause and ignore his business of electric appliances but without letting the control pass on to some one else. Or he may join politics or social work without any successor to his business affairs having taken control. This can happen to those successful entrepreneurs who lose interest in their business as they approach middle age, and apply their tremendous energies to other walks of life. Tragically, they do not delegate the responsibility, of running the business, to others; nor do they groom and nurture a successor. Many instances of this phenomenon are visible in India.

Actions that Induce Sickness

I have elaborated on these causes in the context of small industry management in my earlier book.[1] I recapitulate them here and give examples how they are not necessarily restricted to small industry alone. Conventional wisdom has set ways of classifying industry: household industry, cottage industry, tiny industrial units and small industrial units. This classification is done on the basis of invested capital, employment and use of electrically or mechanically driven equipment. The purpose of this classification is quasi-legal, usually to decide the 'eligibility' of a unit for one or another form of concessional treatment from appropriate state department. I am not interested that aspect at all. In fact in another context, I had contributed to evolving a conceptual continuum

Figure 5.1: The progression of small enterprises

Basic entrepreneurial unit outlined above

↓

A unit which now employs one or two persons, often from the same household

↓

A unit that uses inputs from such units as above or pools their produce for marketing

↓

A small industrial unit in the modern sense with proper manufacturing place and substantial investment

---

[1] Phansalkar, SJ; *How Not to Ruin Your Small Industry*, Response Books, New Delhi, 1996.

of micro and small enterprises. Right at the bottom, we have essentially self-employed persons who operate in a manner that has some entrepreneurial flavour. Self-employed persons choose it often and, perhaps, usually because they do not find 'jobs' or a wage employment of some kind. We may call this a micro-enterprise or livelihood enterprise. Here the 'entrepreneur' seldom employs anyone else, essentially earns enough to feed his family and does not aim at or reinvest in growth.

The spectrum is more clearly visible if one also controls for the locale: rural areas, rural growth centres, peri-urban areas and cities/metros. The exact size per se is not important to me, what is important is that issues on which decisions are made by entrepreneurs have almost the same basic flavour but start becoming more and more complex as one progresses from the very smallest livelihood enterprise to a medium industry. (I shall use the words 'small industry', for this entire continuum.)

Generalisations can be sweeping. Yet, they can be useful in drawing out the lay of the land, keeping in mind that there will be several exceptions to the generalisation made. What follows is based, substantially, on the observations of small industry management in India and, partly, also on a systematic research conducted by a team including myself. I begin by offering some alibi for what will subsequently be considered an uncharitable caricature of small and medium industry management.

One may posit two main classes of entrepreneurs running Small Scale Enterprise (SSE) in India.

- Those who are or began their business life as junior members of an established trading concern and
- Those whose parental families were never in an industry or trade.

The latter start a SSE because they have a technical background, contacts, experience in a specific line, a bit of money and a fire in the belly to start something on their own.

The former category inherits much of the attitudes and thought process of the trader community. The ethos and 'climate of opinions' which breeds these attitudes is discussed in the next chapter.

The second type takes time to be broken into the harsh realities of business finance; they tend to be cocky about their own abilities and expertise. Not used to getting things done on their own, they can flounder on the slippery paths in the regulatory maze. Quite a few small industry units start with a tight working capital that becomes progressively worse. This keeps the entrepreneurs pre-occupied with here and now; immediate and relatively petty issues. To keep cash costs low, they themselves do as much of this fire fighting as possible. Then, they use fixers and brokers to get themselves out of various jams (sales tax, central excise, labour courts, environmental pollution people, income tax, food and drugs people, etc.) They have little time and even lesser inclination to look at their business in perspective. They may often think that long-term strategic thinking is a luxurious waste of time. This preoccupation with the immediate issues remains with them for a long time.

Issue of the Mindset

While most of the management in small and medium industry is in a closely held company format, some of it may be in the process of transition from proprietary or partnership firms to closely held company. Irrespective of the legal structure, the decision-making is highly centralised. Everything has to be approved by the boss. Everyone effectively reports only to him. This can be represented as in Figure 5.2.

Figure 5.2: Highly centralised decision-making

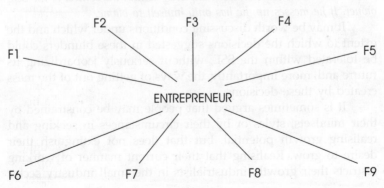

In Figure 5.2, F1, F2, etc. are various functions. Basically, anything and everything moves only when the entrepreneur himself (the senior partner, proprietor, MD—it does not matter what you call him) himself propels it. There is a weak and, often, transient staff at supervisory levels. This reality puts a great deal of strain on the entrepreneur's time and energy. A part of the reason of the state of affairs as well as the strain could be the mindset of the entrepreneur himself, an issue to which we revert later.

Consequently, I have found that entrepreneurs commit or are forced into committing inappropriate management actions. I have bluntly called these inappropriate management actions as blunders. The eight blunders that I have identified are seen to be committed by entrepreneurs across sectors of economy and regions of the country. These are:

- Asset specificity and excessive dependence on one buyer,
- Expanding fixed asset base without providing for enough working capital,
- Speculating on borrowed money,
- Doing informal business,
- Floating many dummy firms to escape regulations,
- Marketing myopia and astigmatism,
- Hiring people for reasons other than their competence,
- Improper project planning that adds to unproductive interest and salary costs.

Table 5.1 attempts to sum up the pathology and consequences of these blunders. *The point to carefully bear in mind is that decisions on all these matters are almost completely within the control of the SSE owner. If he messes up, he has only himself to blame.*

It may be worth discussing conditions under which and the extent to which the decisions suggested in these blunders could be tolerated within the SSE, without seriously jeopardizing its future and, more importantly, the ways of getting out of the mess created by these decisions.

It is sometimes argued that people may be constrained by their mindsets, styles or by their circumstances in seeking and realising growth potential, but that does not extinguish their desire to grow. Realising that their current manner of working restricts their growth, industrialists in the small industry sector

Table 5.1: Blunders SSE owners are prone to commit

Blunder	Logic/Cause/Justification offered by entrepreneurs	Consequences
Asset specificity and excessive dependence on one buyer	Consistent with limited resources, tall promises of vendor development people, contacts with senior management in large industry	Fortunes linked to the buyer, the buyer can squeeze, can exploit and force bankruptcy, may induce obsolescence
Biting off more than you can chew: debt financed expansion of fixed asset base	Usually to tap huge seasonal demand, often induced by easy access to debt instrument caused by good run in the past; also because some trader beckons, working capital is assumed to be manageable	Major liquidity crisis, forcing adoption of poor financing and later purchase and sales practices
Speculating on borrowed money	Familiarity with the commodity, greed and cocky optimism	Utter financial ruin
Doing informal business	Need to generate cash to take care of bribes, greed, myopia, and cocky disregard for regulations	Keeps books in poor shape, cannot grow in a proper manner, and may still face tensions of tax raids
Floating too many dummy firms	Escaping regulations and expenses imposed by them, and evading excise duties	By itself less problematic, but later creative management of accounts of all the 'firmlets' causes the same consequences as above

(contd.)

Table 5.1: contd.

Blunder	Logic/Cause/Justification Offered by entrepreneurs	Consequences
Marketing myopia and astigmatism	Hangover of shortage economy, arrogance and pride in one's products, unwillingness to take a long-term view of markets	Loss of big potential customers, getting stuck in the rut
Hiring people for reasons other than competence	Pressures from neighbours, relations, friends, tax people, government people and so on, diffidence of entrepreneurs to hire and engage with competent professionally trained people	Silly, costly man-made mistakes, reinforcement of the star mode, kitchen politics within the unit, good people never wishing to join
Improper project planning	Insufficient pre-project study of the business	Working capital interest, salaries, depreciation and other overheads pile up before any sales may occur

Source: Phansalkar, SJ; *How not to Ruin Your Small Industry,* Response Books, New Delhi, 1996.

may seek external advice and services. Such service is included in what may be termed business development service, or BDS for short. I had an occasion to study this subject with Prof. MS Sriram.[2] We looked at how small industrialists view the services offered to them, which services do they want, like, can pay for, etc. Based on Ninety structured interactions with SSE in four sectors and nearly a dozen interviews with BDS providers, we concluded the following:

Inputs needed by SSE may be divided in two categories: transaction related services and strategic services. 'Transaction related services' such as those needed to manage accounts, labour laws, almost every SSE needs tax records, returns and compliance with other regulations. While quite a few SSE at the lower end manage even these on their own, a bulk of them uses BDS in this category—at least for the tax and regulations purposes. These inputs are usually obtained from subject matter specialists—including petty functionaries in the regulating agencies them-selves—who may, but need not, restrict their interaction to the relevant transactions. Two sub-categories within these: routine services and specialised services for sorting major problems may be noted, the latter used only when there is a major jam and the provider identified through the routine BDS provider or through the industry association.

Box 5.1: Glossary of terms used in Table 5.1

> **Asset specificity** refers to a situation in which a set of produc-tive assets can be used to make only one product or service of a rigidly defined specification. For instance, instead of getting the main structural frame of a truck chassis forged from outside, Ashok Leyland installed an expensive frame press in their Hosur plant. That machine can produce nothing except truck chassis frames. You may argue that I have asset specificity in that I can pursue only academic pursuits such as reading, writing, teaching and research, but cannot be a good manager.
>
> (Box contd.)

[2] Phansalkar, SJ; and Sriram, MS; 'Business development services for small enterprises—a study of Hyderabad, India, Small Enterprise Development', 12:1, June 2001.

(Box contd.)

Fixed asset is understood in the usual sense of land, buildings, plant and machinery etc. Fixed assets soak a lot of money and the assets can be used for a long time. The fixed assets are seldom 'liquid' and can usually be converted into money only at a huge loss.

Enough working capital is needed for buying and keeping a required level of stock, work-in-progress, finished goods, trade credits and for meeting fixed payout liabilities during the period when sales realisations are not expected. A concept of working capital pipeline is used to assess the working capital needed. We would consider it to be enough when one is able to easily pay all external liabilities most of the time and has no reason to consider any interruption or change in optimal business practices for want of liquid money.

Speculation, while commonly understood, is used in the sense of buying raw materials or hoarding finished goods well beyond the normal level required for a smooth manufacturing process, simply because one expects favourable movement of the price and hence gains on account of price changes.

Informal business is the selling and buying of things, without issuing or asking for bills. Usually these transactions are done in cash and don't enter the firm's books of accounts at all. The profit and loss account of the firm is not affected by these transactions and hence formal sales and profit figures are grossly under-reported.

Dummy firms are firms floated by the same promoters, perhaps having their registered address in the same place, engaged in the very same or some highly related business, sharing the same manufacturing/accounting/sales infrastructure but existing as separate legal entity.

In order to understand what triggers the hiring of professional BDS providers for transaction related issues, we asked the entrepreneurs what would trigger the hiring of consultant. We also asked them to name the source that helps them to identify such providers, and if such providers are hired on a consistent basis. A small number (13 out of 90) reported that they would not hire a BDS provider for any transaction related issue. An overwhelming number (63 out of 77) reported that they would use a BDS provider because of the complexity of the case, and a smaller number (14 out of 77) reported that they would do so if there were serious repercussions or if a significant amount was involved. It can be seen that the responses do not vary across sectors. About half of the respondents who reported that they would not hire BDS providers, belonged to the computer sector. In case BDS providers were to be hired, the SSE depended on friends' circles, business circles and industry associations. Pharma and engineering firms depended more on the business associates/industry associations than the other sectors. It is clear from Table 5.1 that, at least as far as transactions related BDS is concerned, these providers were used on a consistent basis. This may be interpreted as a general level of satisfaction among the BDS providers in this segment.

The 'strategic services' such as those needed with regard to non-immediate or non-urgent issues, but to expand business, identify and service markets, design products, set up facilities and seek finances, are needed by a large number of SSE; though only a few use them. The reasons for their reluctance to use the services of the BDS providers include their mindset, their perception that there is 'no value for money' in this regard, and their awe for strategic BDS providers.

Significantly, areas wherein external assistance was sought were, broadly, two—finance and marketing. This was also confirmed, by some questions, in other parts of the questionnaire—we shall deal with these issues a little later in this book. On most of the other issues, the SSE tended to take a decision on their own, rather than seek outside help.

I now sum up the discussion on behaviour and orientation of the typical small industry owner. The typical small industry owner operates his unit in the star model, wherein he is the central or the only decider in everything that is done in the unit. He is harassed by having too much to do, and is almost always pressed for time. Also, he is usually pressed with the immediate problems of an urgent type. His style of operation seems to be oriented towards decisions based on his judgment from time to time rather than set organisational procedures, absence of delegation, individual hard work rather than teamwork and a degree of suspicion and distrust about others. His environment and compulsions make him prone to commit acts (blunders as I call them) that are decidedly against his long-term interests. He is often engaged in making myriad small changes in the way he carries out his logistical operations. He has no time or inclination to look at strategic aspects. For information and advice on matters pertaining to growth, expansion or new products, he extensively relies either on the family and his social network or on his trusted Chartered Accountant (CA). He uses outside help mainly for enabling him to manage petty, immediate transactions that act as major irritants for him; but seldom uses any other service provider other than the CA, to give him services of a strategic nature.

These actions and behavioural patterns are unique to small industry owners. Let me first look at the blunders, and see if these are also committed by other categories of business units. The combination of asset specificity and excessive dependence on one buyer is to be seen in a wide range of industrial units—small and medium—that work as ancillaries to large companies. It is seen much more in the automobile sector because here the association with one buyer and hence the effect of his performance on the unit are the most demonstrable. Yet, this is also visible in specialized industrial units that produce capital goods such as mining or earth moving products.

Biting off more than you can chew or expanding fixed assets based on borrowed money, and without providing for enough working capital is perhaps the most common of these blunders seen in medium and even large Indian businesses. For example, the ice cream maker Dinshaw expanded his capacity circa year 2000 by borrowing extensively. His ice creams sold very well indeed, but the borrowings induced such a heavy cash outflow for debt servicing that the increased sales did not cover them, and the control of the unit changed hands in favour of the lender. Core Parenterals had a dream run of expansion and commercial success between 1988 and 1993–94. Extremely large investments in fixed assets—such as huge expansion in production facilities including a captive power plant, financed through debts—were among the basic causes that led to the decline in the fortunes of the company, bringing it in the BIFR fold by 1998. Chaturvedi's Flex Industry had almost an identical rise and fall: its fortunes grew to a formidable level with its innovation and the expansion of its flexible packaging business. Massive debts, that financed his investments in BOPP tapes, brought the company in great trouble and eventually to the BIFR.

Marketing myopia and astigmatism are seen far too commonly. For instance, the sedate Dhanvantari Malam[3] held on to its *malam* formulation as the major product well beyond the time when competitors such as HopNskip had changed the nature of the market. It lost precious market-share in a vastly expanding market and is still trying to catch up. While Ghoshal[4] certifies it to be world class, the fact remains that Bajaj betted on *'hamara scooter'* for a shade too long; and suffered, if nothing else, major loss of opportunity in the two-wheeler industry. Possibly its huge reserves' position and its opening of exports markets reduced the pain significantly.

Hiring personnel for reasons other than their competence has been a ubiquitous attribute in Indian business. Social obligations and feeling of security in one's own ilk tended to make Indian businessmen hire from their own community and, sometimes, even the kinship. The resultant pattern of organisational pettiness, sycophancy and disgusting interference with formal authority structures, has been a common phenomenon with a lot of companies in India. Trouble is, even when one wants, one cannot reduce the workforce or take punitive action. I have also discussed the reluctance to hire professional managers in the earlier chapter and that too is a part of this very same mindset. While professionals can be retained or fired on grounds of performance, as Gurucharan Das[5] quotes an industrialist, 'how do you fire a family man?' As education levels across all social strata are improving, the degree of compromise in competence and merit in favour of kinship affinity is perhaps reducing; yet it is better to be on guard as far as this blunder is concerned.

Speculating, doing business informally, creating many dummy firms and creative accounting to reduce net tax liability are patterns of behaviour closely associated with ethics of the business. I have dealt with this matter in the last chapter. It sure does look as if no category of Indian business is free from these blunders.

---

[3] See the case at the end of this chapter.
[4] Ghoshal, S; et. al, op. cit.
[5] Das, Gurucharan; op. cit.

Finally, the comments of Datta about the reliance of the family-managed companies on Cas, referred to in the last chapter, seem to indicate that the pattern of behaviour of the small industry owners with regard to using outside help for furthering their business perhaps extended beyond the small industry sector. This, though, seems to be changing with the times. The trend of hiring internationally reputed management consultants caught on with the large industrial houses in the last decade and, perhaps, will extend to lesser business families through emulative behaviour.

In summary then, the causes of poor performance and sickness discussed above seem to be relevant to Indian business in general.

Dhanvantari Ltd[6]

Evolution of Dhanvantari

Nagendranath Dwiwedi started Dhanvantari as a patent medicine firm in 1892. The firm, then known as Dhanvantari Depot, prepared and sold the herbal *malam* (ointment or a balm) known, throughout the history of the company, as *Dhanvantari Malam* (DM). The firm shifted its production and business headquarters to Jaipur in the early Twenties. The firm was converted into a company in 1936 and, till date, continues to be a closely held company with the family of the promoter holding a majority of the shares. The chief promoter was a patriotic patriarch who stood the high moral ground. He was associated with the Gandhian movement and was the preferred host of the Mahatma whenever the latter visited Jaipur. He also supported several public causes. The company's *malam* had become a household name and, in one of its brand recall surveys, DM was among the most frequently recalled Indian brands, competing with Amul and Bajaj. Dhanvantari had two factories: the older one in Jaipur and the other in Agra established in 1975. In 1977, Dhanvantari added an R&D centre. In 1988, it established a finance subsidy that offered 'total financial solutions'. It set up an herbal, fine chemicals extraction unit in 1989. In 1996, it established two separate

---

[6] Identities disguised. Ananthnarayana Sarma prepared the original case.

companies—the unit that supplied its packaging materials to Dhanvantari was hived off into a subsidiary company, and a leather-processing unit was established. In 1998, it established an Infotech division within its finance subsidiary, and in 2002 it was planning to establish a call centre in the local software technology park.

In 1991–92, of its total sales of Rs 23 crores, Rs 22 crores came from *malams*. It sold three variants of DM, in three packing sizes then. The company held on to its product formulations and also added inhalers and lozenges drops in the OTC category. It also sold fine chemicals. In 1999–2000, the company had reached a sales turnover of Rs 64 crores, of which Rs 52 crores came from the *malam*. In 1999–2000, the printing subsidiary made a loss of nearly six crores on a turnover of Rs 20 crores. The finance subsidiary that had an income of Rs 25 crores was also profusely bleeding during that year.

Manufacturing and Logistics at Dhanvantari

The manufacture of DM was a straightforward process of mixing herbal extracts (essential oils) with base materials, and packing the mixtures thus prepared. The following steps were involved in the process:

a) Active ingredient preparation (eight essential oils)
   – Manual mixing in a plastic drum.
b) Base material melting
   – Various waxes taken in a steam jacket machine for melting.
c) Mixing base material with active ingredients
   – When the base material reached a particular temperature, the active ingredients were pumped into steam jacket machine and mixed mechanically.
d) Filling it in the requisite packaging
   – The *malam* is received at the filling stations in a liquid form. Separate filling machines exist for bottles, liquids, plastic sachets and tins.
e) Capping
   – Machines were used for capping filled bottles and tins.
f) Packaging the bottle in the pack

- Bottle packaging in a printed soft cardboard pack. This
   had been mechanised for the nine gram DM bottle. The
   rest was done manually.
g) Packing in plastic cartons for despatch
   - The final products had to be packed in plastic pouches,
   each containing 20 units. This had been mechanised for
   the nine-gram bottle.

This simple technology evolved over a period of time. As machines for different operations became available, Dhanvantari
adopted them. For instance, it adopted a melting and mixing vat
with a steam heating jacket; instead of the earlier gas heated vat
in early Eighties. It also shifted to electronic filling and weighing
systems for its major product the nine-gram DM. That line also had
a mechanised unit for packing the bottles in cartons. However,
other product manufacturing had not undergone any change. It
still continued to use a batch processing method of production for
the main product. It had a pre-eminent position in the market in
the pain relieving OTC medicine category, but it was not the first
to introduce the spray introduced by its two major competitors—
Ideax and *HopNskip*. It did not effect any change in the manufacturing technology since the Nineties. The other products were also
simple. The company had three factories in all: the original factory
at Jaipur and the new one at Agra made DM. The third factory,
located at Kareli near Jaipur, made packaging materials and other
products. The same premises also housed the unit for manufacture
of bulk drugs. The latter was initially set up as an R&D unit for
herbal products but is now used for making bulk drugs.

The cost of production was dominated by materials' cost, 30
per cent of which was accounted for by bottles and essential oils
each. These essential oils are agro-based materials. The major
items were menthol (30 per cent) eucalyptus (20 per cent), lemon
grass (10 per cent) and turpentine (6 per cent). The first harvest
for these items was usually in the April–June season, and this
created seasonal fluctuations in pricing. Dhanvantari gave rate
contracts to suppliers for material with monthly pricing schedule.
It was interesting to note that despite almost a century of continuous engagement in the use of these agro-based materials, the
company had not introduced backward integration into the processing of herbs to produce essential oils.

Marketing at Dhanvantari

Two, very senior executives with marketing experience in marketing of FMCG and OTC products, managed the marketing operations at Dhanvantari. DM was essentially herbal remedy for headache, muscle sprain and body aches; and belonged to the category known to industry circles as 'rubs and balms'. Patent medicines, traditional preparations and OTC products comprised most of this category. The total market size in this category was estimated at about Rs 450 crores. Other brands of herbal balms included *Ideax*, *HopNskip* and *Marigold*. The market was growing only demographically, at about 5 per cent per year. While the approximate market share of Vicks was 20 per cent, was 15 per cent for DM and that for *Marigold*, *HopNskip*, and *Ideax* was about 12 per cent each; smaller, regional brands shared the remaining market share. Competitors introduced alternate pack sizes. While the market in the south preferred small packs and sachets, the market in the west had somehow taken to larger pack sizes. In fact, the States that were more prosperous and had witnessed greater westernisation consumed less of the product, and preferred substitutes such as sprays. Analgesic and anti-inflammatory products such as *Combiflam* and other non-herbal products often used for symptoms such as muscle sprain and body aches. In the mid-Nineties, sprays using about the same ingredients had come in vogue and had been additionally projected as 'quick acting and convenient' products. *HopNskip* and *Ideax* were seen on the shelf more commonly.

The market for OTC, pain-relieving products was essentially driven by the distribution chain. The distribution chain followed by Dhanvantari was in keeping with the industry trend. The flow of goods was from the factory to 130 C&F agents and, then, to the wholesalers and retailers. Dhanvantari had nearly 2000 wholesalers in the year 2000, compared to half that number a decade ago. The product was on the shelves of about 350000 retail outlets. It was said to be particularly strong in Rajasthan, UP, Punjab and Haryana regions. Dhanvantari offered a commission of 15 per cent to retailers and 8 per cent to wholesalers against the commission of 30 per cent and 10 per cent respectively offered by *Marigold*. The industry norm was for about 10 per cent commission to wholesalers and 20 per cent to retailers. Dhanvantari felt that a lower commission was adequate for its extremely strong brand.

Dhanvantari assessed that the market for its own DM was mainly in the middle-income segment. Youngsters did not like the strong smell of DM that lingered on and the oily-sticky feeling it gave. *HopNskip*, in particular, had adopted an aggressive marketing stance with heavy accent on promotion. Its ad campaigns targeted the 30 something, modern, Indian woman prone to backaches. The fact that herbal, pain-relieving products had a rustic image and were not considered fashionable, was recognized by all. *Ideax*, on the other hand, had tried to capture the market of the athletic younger set. Its ad campaigns always had an element of sports in them. Both Marigold and Dhanvantari were older companies and had established reputations in their respective regions: Dhanvantari in the north and Marigold in the west. However, unlike Dhanvantari, Marigold had a range of ayurvedic and herbal products. In their advertisements, both these companies kept stressing on the brand names, and the fact that they were trusted over generations. While the promotion budget for Dhanvantari was barely 8 per cent of its sales, the same for *HopNskip* was said to be four times the same in rupee terms. *Vicks* and *Ideax* spent almost three times more on their promotion, than what Dhanvantari spent. Most of this budget was spent on TV commercials, in the Nineties. Dhanvantari used its promotion budget to support 'socially desirable things' that it thought were befitting its redoubtable nationalism and proud past. For example, in the Eighties when DD was the only channel available, Dhanvantari sponsored the Saturday afternoon film slot that showed award-winning, regional films or other such 'art' films. In the north, it sponsored 'family' type serials.

Finance in Dhanvantari

Dhanvantari was a closely held company, held so by the Dwiwedi family. The company was formed in 1936, with the first issue of some 500000 shares of Rs 100 each. No fresh equity has been issued in its 67 years. However, bonus shares were issued a number of times. Till the early Nineties, over 90 per cent of its shares was held by the Dwiwedi family and its close relatives. The shareholding had become more widely held, and the family owned no more than 58 per cent shares. 9000 investors held the balance shares. The shares were not very liquid as there was hardly any transaction happening on them. The company had taken debt twice, in the form of secured debentures; but there was hardly any outstanding debt left. Against the owner's equity of Rs 196 million in the year 2001, for instance, the outstanding borrowings amounted to only Rs 87 million—of which Rs 24 million were by way of deposits from stockists and fixed deposits from the public. In that year, Dhanvantari made a profit of Rs 61 million on a sales turnover of Rs 640 million, and had a positive cash flow of Rs 110 million. The company had started taking large deposits from the stockists and had now reduced the trade debtors to 23 days of sales now, from an earlier level of over 85 days of sales. Dhanvantari had invested surplus cash in Dhanvantari Finance, the company that claimed to offer 'complete financial solutions' and engaged mainly in lease finance business since the year 1987. While it made good money in the first few years, the stock market bust of 1992 and the downturn later meant that the finance company was left with a lot of non-performing assets. The company had invested over Rs 200 million in the finance company and had also taken deposits from the public for lending it to its borrowers. A surge in NPA and continuous fall in interest rates had seen this investment turning into a nightmare.

Research and Development at Dhanvantari

In 1977, Dhanvantari established its R&D laboratory at Kareli. A reputed scientist from one of the prestigious Indian laboratories was brought in to head the laboratory. He was very well-known in the research field connected to phytochemistry of herbal products. While the R&D centre did not bring about any new preparation nor made any process change during the six years of his tenure, the scientist brought laurels to the laboratory through a number of research papers published in internationally reputed journals. Dhanvantari thought that this was very good indeed and reinforced its image of a responsible and respected company. After this famous scientist, Dr Mishra, retired, the laboratory was asked to focus on three areas of research: isolation of active ingredients in herbal materials, fine chemicals and synthetic product formulations. It undertook contract research in herbal medicine on behalf of about foreign companies and this had enabled the company to earn revenue of some two million rupees in the year 2001.

Human Resource Management at Dhanvantari

The Dwiwedis believed that, since the God had been kind to them and had given them a great deal of wealth and comfort, it was incumbent upon them to help people from their community and from their district by employing them. As such, a majority of the administrative staff and workmen came from the same clan as the Dwiwedis. Their kinship network among the staff was complex and stretched a long way; so much that, in some sense, each *pai* belonging to the staff members was related if one delved deep enough. The Dwiwedi family was, of course, regarded as superior to all the others; and the social hierarchy was judged from how 'closely related' someone was to their family. Compared to the wage and benefits package in the pharma line, the company package appeared frugal. Of course, there was a low-key, grumbling feeling about this, but no one ever articulated it much. This was because of the whole approach to human resource management. The company provided for all the possible needs of the staff: health, housing loans, children's education, family obligations such as daughter's marriage, etc. by designing suitable employee policies. These included a whole combination of 'assured welfare schemes', 'incentives', staff loans, and of course emergency or special grants wherever warranted and deserving. To top it all, fresh recruitment to the categories of junior administrative and workmen were done only from among the wards or close relations of the existing staff. Thus, everyone expected to have at least one of his children to be employed in Dhanvantari after s/he retired, and reasonably so. However, officers and marketing staff were hired on the basis of their qualifications and experience and not on the basis of clan. Most of the staff attrition was concentrated in these senior, professional categories and occurred mainly when the person was not from the same social set.

New Businesses at Dhanvantari

The Dwiwedis were seen to be somewhat quixotic. A business journal reported that Dwiwedis' business decisions seemed to follow the flavour of the period, rather than any concerted game plan. In the Eighties' lease finance boom, the Dwiwedis set up the 'total finance company'. Later, in the smaller booms of the early Nineties, they toyed with assorted export-oriented lines such as leather and granite. The run up to the new century saw the Dwiwedis first setting up an IT training firm and, then, a software development unit. In the year 2001, they announced their desire to set up a 30 seat Call Centre. Some of these were set up as separate companies, some as units under one of the other companies; and a nephew or a son-in-law of one of the Dwiwedis usually headed them. In its core business, the company sales were growing only demographically.

How had Dhanvantari Fared?

At Dhanvantari, the sales had tripled from about 190 million in 1991 to Rs 640 million over the decade of the Nineties. Almost 80 per cent of this was from the DM range. This hid the deep slide in the company's market-share of pain-relievers, rubs and ointments. The sales of HopNskip had shot up by a factor of 10 during the same time, on the back of its more trendy advertisements: sometimes a very good looking, modern Indian housewife, sometimes a 40 something executive out to impress his female colleague and, at other times, robust young men playing a good athletic game. Dhanvantari continued to nurture its self-image of a patriotic, socially responsible and respectable business house. It continued to contribute to charities for promotion of Indian culture such as classical music and dance. All visitors were told of how the Mahatma accepted their hospitality each time he came to that town. Perhaps, the company management found the present so revolting and depressing that they preferred to live in the past.

OPPORTUNITIES AND STRATEGIES FOR INDIAN BUSINESS

Following a brief look-back at the economic changes that occurred during the decade I have discussed six issues so far.

- I have looked at how did Indian industry cope with these changes.
- I offered a categorisation of strategic and opportunistic behaviour.
- I discussed at some length the way Indian family business tends to function and the challenges it faces.
- I explained at length the pattern that can properly be called strategic business behaviour.
- I then went on to sum up the lessons from research on the patterns of behaviour that are associated with good performance—whether in terms of quick, and sustained growth, or in terms of coping with challenges of liberalisation.
- I also offered a detailed discussion on the causes of stagnation and sickness.

In Chapter four, we saw that sound performers exhibited a cluster of attributes. I sum these up for a quick recap:

- Sound performers tend to choose products at the start of its PLC.

  This indicates a high degree of professional commitment to the chosen field, confidence in one's judgment as well as willingness to take risk. It also indicates that the company management has thought about the future, expects that the chosen product line will do well in it and hence has taken steps to plan for it.
- They tend to focus on improving efficiency of operations, as shown in lower inventories, smaller credit periods to buyers and superior margins. These efficiencies come from combination of things. Improvement in efficiencies requires sustained attention to business details. This means that the management takes more interest in the nitty-gritty of the business, and does not confine itself to management of money alone. Superior product margins come from focusing on high-end products, as much as it does from cost reduction. When one puts the first point, about choosing products at the start of their PLC, vis-à-vis the point about superior product margins, we come to the conclusion that superior performance has to result not from me-too products and even less so from management of commodity like businesses; but from well-positioned, possibly niche but growing products that take a lot of time in choosing, evolving and developing.
- Sound performers tend to evolve a competitive advantage through bootstrapping. Also sound performers develop innovations in operating technology. These two features again indicate great application of mind to the business processes themselves, and not to issues (such as regulation, taxation etc.) that surround them.
- Sound performers exhibit proactive behaviour in most fields of the business, but notably in the product-market arena. Rather than waiting for changes to happen before it reacts, the business anticipates and attempts to make the changes it wants.
- Sound performers tend to veer round to conservative financing decisions. They tend to bring down the total leverage sharply, rely more on internal accruals and tend to use these for the financing of working capital.

Chapter five suggests that the main reasons for keeping a business stagnant and possibly heading it towards sickness, deal with eight blunders: excessive dependence on one buyer, expanding fixed assets without providing for enough working capital, speculation on borrowed money, falling a prey to greed in doing informal business, floating dummy firms to take advantage of regulatory gaps and then getting enmeshed in complex accounting to reduce tax liability, hiring for reasons other than employee competence, etc. Reasons for stagnation also deal with complacence about one's products and its telltale, pristine, paramount position as well as with the somewhat peculiarly Indian attribute of over-diversifying and, hence, spreading cash resources thin (if not squandering) over a large number of businesses chosen because either they happen to be fashionable or because they help the family settle one of the young scions. Trying out a large number of lines is not so much an issue as trying them out for some extraneous reason (such as availing of some fiscal or regulatory advantage) and not following any of them through till it yields success.

I now return to the questions I raised in the introduction to this book. They are:

A

Did Indian companies behave 'strategically' at all during this time (the time of rapid changes in economic environment)? Or were they essentially opportunistic? Who behaved strategically and who behaved opportunistically? Can one associate better performance with strategic response?

B

How do Indian businesses look at changes in their environments? Do they behave like vested interests that feel threatened with such changes and hence react to forestall, obviate, deflect, dilute or blunt these changes?

C

What determines how a specific business behaves when faced with rapidly changing, economic environment?

The first question relates to the nature of response exhibited by Indian companies to changes in economic environment. One may start by exploring whether strategic behaviour has a place in the Indian business environment at all, or does somewhat deliberate opportunism double up as strategy? Whether one likes it or not, the very question is loaded. It assumes that 'strategic behaviour' which conforms to the textbook formulations on strategy (sharp product-market definitions, growth vector that neatly makes a logical connection to the product-market definition, a competitive advantage that is rooted in solid attributes of business and a well-marked synergy across multiple business units) is desirable; a sort of standard benchmark towards which all business behaviour ought to tend, and against which it can be tested. I do not wish to take such a peremptory and rigid position. I recognise that too sharp a focus in business in an emergent and turbulent environment is perhaps not warranted. In the introduction to this book I have also recognised that, for decades, Indian business environment was over-constraining and hence created an ethos that did not encourage businesses to act strategically in this sense. That is precisely why this question, whether deliberate opportunism has been doubling up as strategy in India, becomes more relevant. Least of all, the data about how the companies responded to the changes in economic environment in terms of products, markets, business practices, organisation changes, etc., as summed up in Tables 4.1–4.23, is a good base to judge whether the Indian businesses behaved strategically and whether this was related to performance. There of course remains the danger that one will give a trivial answer: those who performed well behaved strategically and those who faltered did so because of their opportunism.

I take a close look at these tables again. From Table 4.2 and Table 4.3, we see that more 'well performing companies' introduced many new products and earlier on, than the companies that faltered. Table 4.4 shows that most of the high performers introduced products that were related to their existing businesses—either by way of integration or by way of product extension. Only one high performer introduced a wholly new product during the Nineties. They, the high performers, greatly expanded the product volume. They reduced the credit periods and often 'outsourced' distribution, by shifting to the C&F system from the earlier Company Depot system (Table 4.5–Table 4.7). They also relied more on the outsourcing of the products they sold (Table 4.11). Most of them adopted steps to obtain ISO certification or its equivalent and had adopted greater automation for more efficient operations (Tables 4.17 and 4.18). Thus it appears plausible to me, to state that at least a section of the Indian businesses behaved 'strategically'. At the same time, we have narrated the reality pertaining to unrelated, opportunistic diversification as being the norm rather than the exception during the same period.

The second question is about the essential outlook of the businesses to changes. I think I have provided enough indicative data about this. A substantial part of the Indian businesses have behaved like vested interest groups, they have tried hard to obviate changes. Bombay Club is an example of that. They have cried foul when they perceived new entrants having greater advantages. They, particularly the small industry sector, have sought continuance of old, cozy policies of subsidies; preferred purchase norms and product reservations. They have resisted liberalisation in imports. Yet, a small section of the Indian industry, notably the first generation entrepreneurs from the category (d) of 'non-business family entrepreneur run businesses' (see Chapter two) have taken the liberalisation process at flood. They have dared, looked their global competitor in the eye and have, at times, made the latter wilt.

The third question relates to the determinants of response and behaviour. Like S Roy,[1] we too have reported in our research that young, stand-alone companies are likely to exhibit proactive, strategic behaviour rather than the businesses owned and controlled by established business families. In the first place, a young stand-alone business is probably manned by professionals who are technically and business-wise on top of things; and has, perhaps, tried to get the team style of working in its routines. So, it finds it easier to bounce ideas about the future and to evolve plans to put them in action. Second, they have greater freedom and energy to act. If one had to introduce Weiner's cat in this context, the small, young and stand-alone business is like an alert and nimble cat, the sort of cat from which no prey is safe. It has not yet added extra tiers around its waistline. The business is too young to have any deadwood. On the other hand, businesses of old and established business families are likely to be like a cat

---

[1] S Roy, op. cit.

of slow, settled habits which has been, since long, used to laying an emphasis on stability rather than on speed. The business organisation is likely to have a battalion of men who joined the entrepreneur for reasons of kinship based loyalty, worked with him with dedication, performing mostly non-technical tasks, earned his esteem and trust and consequently rose in the hierarchy of the business group without any corresponding rise in their capabilities. The group of men working in these businesses for long tend to preach age-old and possibly outdated maxims in the style of elaborating on the obvious, and feel insecure about new things and new environments. Having worked in the almost decidedly feudal, paternalistic working style of the Great Patron, they are likely to feel perplexed when asked to think of the future. They are quite likely to try and conjure up how the Great Patron, possibly long gone, would have thought and acted. As the younger scion tries to run the business in a manner that befits the times and not merely the family traditions, he finds their presence a little jarring. Yet Gurucharan Das's[2] question, 'How do you fire a family man?' keeps haunting him and he labours under their weight.

Is Opportunism the Primary Cause of Stagnation and Failure?

Now I have established enough background to make the two main points that I wish to make. In the first place, I suggest that the businesses and the entrepreneurs whose business decision-making exhibits strategic rather than opportunistic orientation have tended to do well, grown and thrived despite adverse turns of events and environment. And the businesses that have opportunistic behaviour have generally shown patchy, inconsistent and usually short-term successes. The second point is that Indian family businesses tend to show opportunistic rather than strategic behaviour and that is the fundamental reason why they have fallen back and taken a beating in the recent years. The rest of this chapter is devoted to an elaboration of these two points.

---

[2] Das, Gurucharan; op. cit.

Let us first see why opportunism in business is generally closer to the causes of stagnation and failure. Naïve opportunism (of the 'taxi driver at the railway station overcharging a fare otherwise unfamiliar to the city' type) is of course uncommon, though not rare in serious business. Most businesses have a vision that stretches beyond a few days if not a few months. But there are less opprobrious shades of opportunism that we saw: taking advantage of changes in administrative prices to make stock profits, following quickly with a me-too concoction when a new product is seen to be a hit; going to the very limit of stretching interpretation of legal points, entering a new field of activity just because everyone else is doing it, cornering licenses and tying up potential resources, taking advantage of weak governance and enforcement of laws etc. Of course, a thousand shades of dishonourable behaviour were rampant in business (black marketing of cement, scooters, caustic soda or whatever else that was in short supply, selling goods of patently shoddy quality and disclaiming responsibility or taking refuge in facelessness, selling goods by charging taxes to customers without paying these to the State and so on) in the past and seen, once in a while, even today. Then there is the morally impeccable but still opportunistic set of acts like speculating on price rises, speculating in securities and real estate, etc. Finally, we have this unique opportunism of over-diversification of a mercantile capitalist that is so common in Indian family business.

Over and above the eight blunders identified by the causes of stagnation and failures in business, the last few chapters included some more: an excessive preoccupation with current and immediate transactions, complacence with the success achieved by the product in the past, and resultant reluctance to change; focussing on smart accounting or financing decisions rather than product performance as a source of profit, excessive diversification and attempting to man the key positions in the business entirely by the men in the family or kinship. It does not take too much analysis or insight to show the conceptual links between these causes of failure and stagnation and opportunism. Doing informal business, speculating on borrowed money, and floating a great deal of dummy firms to reduce liabilities under diverse laws is obviously in the realm of opportunistic behaviour. Interestingly, one of the most common causes of business failure, namely investing too much in fixed assets without providing for adequate working capital, is not a part of the opportunistic behaviour one sees in mercantile capitalists of this country. Perhaps because their approach is like that of mercantile capitalists, they recognise the value of staying liquid and solvent as long as they do not seek voluntary sickness! The tendency to focus on transactions rather than pay attention to product attributes and strategic business issues is perhaps born of a more short-term view of things. This short-term view certainly indicates an orientation that is different from the one needed for patience and the vision needed for strategic behaviour. This may also border on myopia but need not necessarily indicate opportunism. The reluctance to seek strategic inputs from the service providers is indicative of secretive and distrustful behaviour or an absence of openness and transparency. Yet, it could also indicate preference of sharing information on a strictly need-to-know basis. Finally, the tendency to man key positions by family men has perhaps three distinct motivations. The first is to ensure that the family is gainfully engaged. And what better way to do this than to engage in managing the family business itself? The second motivation is to ensure that the goodies of the business are shared within the family and not spent on outsiders. The more this relates to the informal cash earnings, the greater it smacks of opportunism. But this feeling per se may not be born of opportunism as such. Finally, the third and the most critical motivation is to keep 'business secrets' or 'specific knowledge about the business' within the family itself. It has almost no relationship with opportunism.

The inference that emerges is that the roots of several causes of avoidable failures of businesses lie in an essentially opportunistic outlook of the entrepreneur or the business owners. What is perhaps even more pertinent is that these behaviours are quite antithetical to the ingredients of success and sound performance.

Next, I examine the relationship between the ingredients of success and a sound performance with strategic behaviour. These ingredients are: choice of product at the start of its PLC, drive towards efficient operations, financing decisions that progressively reduce leverage, innovations in operating technology, competitive edge based on bootstrapping, proactive behaviour in all business spheres but more particularly in the product-market sphere, a shift from individual decision-making to a team mode of work and a shift towards transparency, systematisation and good governance.

My comments about the tendency to keeping things within the family being antithetical to behaviours that seem to be associated with success should be quite clear from the point about team mode of work. One needs to understand and appreciate this point properly. Family members may remain heads of organisations as they perhaps must; on account of stake-holding. The transition is in approach from a feudal-paternalistic way of managing things to a team based way of managing things. In the former, what the boss says is always right and must be obeyed because he is the boss. He is the boss because he is from the family. In the second, the boss is perhaps still from the family but he knows his limits quite explicitly and creates team-based mechanisms for decision-making. In such teams he is perhaps only one member and sometimes not even that. An example of this is perhaps the shift in the role played by Vikram Lal in his Eicher group of companies. Second, the decision process is dominated by a much greater exchange of views based on information and knowledge; and not mere opinions and instinctive judgment. It is also a possibility that a small core of senior persons, possibly including, or exclusively, men from the family will eventually exercise their instinctive judgment after the analysis part is over. This too is inevitable. Yet, this still differs from the earlier mode characterised by all round presence and dominance of the family men who could invite outside opinions at their sole discretion. Then again the transparency, systematisation and good governance aspects seem to be somewhat removed from the secretive 'family men' dominated culture and also quite removed from the opportunistic mindset.

The factors that are associated with successful coping seem to be at variance with the business behaviour of the conventional business—particularly of the family-managed businesses in India. At the risk of leaning too far, I suggest the following contrast between the typical business behaviour of an average Indian family business with the factors that were associated with successful growth and coping (see Table 6.1).

Table 6.1: Contract of typical Indian family business with factors for successful coping and growth

S. no.	Aspect	Typical orientation of a conventional family business	Behaviour associated with successful coping and growth
1	Choice of products	Established products, often of the me-too type	High end products, possibly niche products
2	Competitive tools	Price discounts and long credit periods	Features and quality aspects of the product
3	Method of selling	Own field force, perhaps a privately held marketing company	Often outsourcing as much as possible high commissions but zero credit
4	Employment pattern	Many and kinship related employees	Fewer and professionally superior employees
5	Essential emphasis	Market-share, possibly speculation, smart accounting	Technical superiority, efficient logistics, product superiority
6	Financing	Debt based, high leverage	Accrued surplus based, low leverage

Ingredients of success and sound performance are certainly far removed from opportunism. Let me take up the point about the choice of products. Opportunistic businesses tend to be more 'me-too' followers while strategic businesses may start the trend by identifying, evolving and introducing products at the start of their life-cycle or starting a new product category altogether. Second, a certain technical and professional competence and confidence is essential to take a bold stand either on innovating and introducing or on choosing a product that is not me-too. As we find, opportunist businessmen do not mind taking financial risks, but are quite unlikely to take risks when it comes to these matters. Let me turn to the aspect of efficiency of operations. There is nothing inherently contradictory between emphasis on continuous improvement in efficiency and opportunism. However, the former requires constant attention to a myriad details that together result in improvement in efficiency. An opportunistic businessman is more likely to find more profitable uses—the way he sees them— for the same time. At times, we saw how the senior management personnel of large traditional companies spent time engaged in insider trading of their stock, rather than soil their hands with the absorbing details of the nitty-gritty of the business that would lead to improvements in efficiency. Both, innovations in operating technology and competitive edge through bootstrapping, are clearly the results of sustained efforts perhaps personally led if not just encouraged and rewarded by a management dedicated to that line of business. In fact assiduous, sustained and nose-to-the grind work required for both these ingredients of success appear to be quite remote from mindset of opportunism. I think there is an organisational schizophrenia in many Indian firms. One component of the organisation is engaged in doing this kind of hard work to gain stability and long-term strength. Simultaneously, another set of people, perhaps at a higher level, is engaged in essentially smart acts of accounting and such other opportunistic behaviour. Such firms certainly engage in opportunistic adventures (such as setting up a firm to try and grab every possible opportunity, taking advantage of tax laws while pushing the legal interpretations to the limits of acceptability, and so on) yet protect their core strength. Thus, hardnosed and prosaic determination to improve operations can, and does, co-exist with treasury opportunism as I defined it and in fact may provide the basic instincts for strategic opportunism as well. There is no harm in either.

Harm is in the opportunistic mindset. To formulate and chalk out strategic initiatives that span a few years, I think that a great deal of thinking, forward planning and analysis is needed. Such analysis and forward planning needs teamwork among specialists, transparency within a fairly extended team and certainly a great deal of formalisation for smooth coordination. On the other hand, opportunistic forays have to be executed quickly before too many competitors and potential adversaries know about it. Thus, there is a degree of contradiction between these two. Again, we may find simultaneous existence of both these tendencies in Indian firms.

To use pictorial representations, I believe that the intersection between opportunistic orientation and causes of failures is very high as shown in Figure 6.1.

Figure 6.1: Causes of failure vis-à-vis opportunism

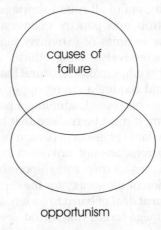

The intersection between strategic orientation and ingredients of success and sound performance is also quite high, as shown in Figure 6.2.

Figure 6.2: Strategic behaviour vis-à-vis success

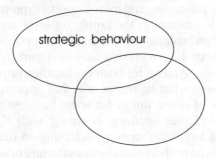

The point I make is that it is not as if a firm is either only opportunistic or purely strategic. There may be simultaneous existence of both these trends in the organisations.

Do We Expect Things to Change?

As we saw in Chapter two, Indian business evolved out of mercantile capitalism and also out of subjugation to British mercantile capitalists. Indian business evolved through phases of extremely anti-business polity, era of all round shortages, all encompassing bureaucratic controls and paucity of investible capital. Indian businessmen grew in times of extremely high marginal rates of taxation and progressively falling ethical standards in public administration. This ethos makes it natural that the classical Indian businessmen would acquire a strong opportunistic orientation.

It is easy to go overboard, adopting a harsh moralistic stand about opportunism. It must be realised that buccaneer capitalism is perhaps an inevitable phase in evolution of a classical capitalist society. Robber barons are not unknown in other parts of the world. In fact concerns for corporate responsibility emerged essentially from revulsion of the society for the capitalist robber barons who often did a great deal of harm to society around them. Recent developments of mega frauds (the sordid developments that saw utter destruction of a very reputed firm of auditors) in American and European corporations clearly show that the phase of selfish opportunism is not really over even in the more advanced countries. Thus, even if one were to agree to the 'flying geese' arguments about business evolution, then one must confront a phase of opportunism in business in India.

The more interesting and more important question is whether opportunism is inherent in the family business and whether the essentially Indian business will step out of its opportunistic grounding? In a seminar I gave on this subject, a participant raised an interesting point: 'What if, for business families, opportunism was strategy?' I guess what he meant was that opportunism may be the usual way of doing things for some business families. They may neither feel that anything is wrong with it, nor feel the necessity for a long-term strategy. Adapting an old adage, long-term strategists have short-term business tenure or so these people may think. While this can of course be true for some, a lot of families are seen to be making the 'right' noises and taking 'copy book' steps such as defining and emphasising their core businesses, hiving off non-core businesses, inducting professionals in the Board, decentralizing and broad-basing decision-making at divisional or similar levels, adapting to e-tools of all sorts, etc. Above all, they seem to be appointing high profile consultants— this day business *brahmins*—to bless them with their hallowed mark of approvals. Thus externally there seems to be signs of a wave of change that began about a decade ago. Three factors connected with the economic policy seem to be driving this general shift. In the first place, reduction in tariffs is reducing protection as surely as reduction of controls while setting up businesses in India is increasing competition. In this changed scenario, scope for opportunistic behaviour is fast reducing. Second, the same changes that threaten the comfortable security of businesses also offer huge scope for ambitious businessmen to move on to the global stage and be noticed at the world level. Finally, the generational transition in the leadership of a family businesses is, itself, introducing changes in the way they will do businesses in future. Yet, it must be realised that these factors of change will take sometime to change mindsets. We must confront the sad fact that in the State as well as business sectors in India, governance is still weak and enforcement pathetic. Insider trading and living with conflicts of interests are perhaps more common than one would like to see. Lax enforcement makes the scope for unsavoury opportunistic behaviour too large for comfort. Till these temptations remain, not all the scions of industry will feel the need to change their orientations. One may possibly expect huge changes in behaviour and orientations in the very large business families, and reducing levels of change as the business volume of the impugned families falls till one reaches mere tokenism if that at the level of business families controlling minor businesses worth may be a few, hundred crore rupees.

Some Propositions

By combining the orientation of the company management (whether on opportunistic-strategic or on proactive-reactive continuum) with the nature and severity of external triggers, I develop some propositions.

These triggers may be of such nature that corporate management may find it completely unable to deal with the situation they indicate. For instance, a small bulk drug manufacturer— when confronted with the product patent regime from 2006—will perhaps believe that it is not possible for him to go on, since he has no capability to invent new molecules anyway, and the old way of 'reverse engineering' is no longer tenable for the bulk drugs demanded. How he responds may depend on his orientation. Other intervening variables would be the financial and technical muscle at his disposal, his commitment to the line of bulk drugs, the options he may perceive, and so on. Essentially, the triggers tell him about the likely competitive structure of the industry he will be in, post–2006. The same conclusion that the triggers tend to the influence the perception about likely competition and profitability of the industry, of the company, is true for other industries as well. The contingency table (Table 6.2) suggests our basic proposition, namely:

'Degree of proactive orientation of management primarily determines the pattern of firm's response when the external environment undergoes fundamental and irrevocable shifts.'

Table 6.2: Patterns of behaviour

	Message of the triggers as interpreted by the management	
	Environment becoming unmanageable, falling profits	Environment severe, but profits attractive.
Reactive management	Pattern I	Pattern II
Proactive management	Pattern III	Pattern IV

Pattern I

The Sulking *Sethji*

The managements of many firms find the environment becoming increasingly disagreeable to them. They find that their industry and certainly more so the way they have been doing business all these days, is no longer attractive when it comes to their long-term profit potential. This situation perhaps applies to a fair number of industries and a very large number of firms that existed in India almost entirely because of the props they received due to government policy. They only inherent competitive strength they had were their ability to manoeuvre the government and manipulate the government officers. As a ready example, one may say that the whole large groups of surviving 'mini' steel, cement or paper mills find themselves in this situation. The management in all these units need not have an orientation of the reactive type. Those who have will exhibit this pattern of behaviour that we name 'The Sulking *Sethji*'. We hypothesise that such reactive management in these firms would be headed/controlled by the 'lizard'[3] type of entrepreneur. This entrepreneur specialises in low technology, and mediocre quality product that is needed for large and regular volumes. He cuts corners where he can. He is unostentatious, unglamorous, *desi*. He is often viewed as myopic and rapacious in dealing with individual customers since his primary mandate is to sell run-of-the-mill kind of products to run-of-the-mill kind of customers. The lizard does not fight but believes in taking shelter behind things to survive in the long run. Survival, and not sizzling growth, is his mission. The reactive CEO heading the management of a large firm, in the situation described in Pattern I is perhaps essentially a much larger lizard. The lizard now finds that his familiar shelters are simply unable to protect him from the powerful predators. And he has not found many other defense mechanisms. So what can he do but sulk? He starts cursing the economic policy and labour legislation that prevents closures and sell-off. He, perhaps, tries to be too smart by half and stage-manages a prolonged strike that naturally deals a crippling blow to his unit. This allows him to exit without any sense of guilt. He is then free to set up a chain of beauty parlours or furniture shops!

Pattern II

Return of the Prodigal Trader

The management in this situation of Pattern II is reactive; in the sense that they respond to changes rather than attempt to formulate a coherent plan that is driven by themselves. Yet, since the industry remains attractive, the management does not want to withdraw and exit either. Often, such an industrialist finds himself

---

[3] Phansalkar, SJ; *How Not to Ruin Your Small Industry*, Response Books, 1996.

unable to create or muster abilities or strengths to compete with the now global players in the new arena. So, the next best thing the management can do, is—you guessed it—'if you cannot beat them, join them!' The management rushes to form joint ventures, strategic alliances, just plain marketing tie-ups, get what they can from the situation. If the firms are really devoid of strengths that are needed in the changed circumstances, eventual exit is perhaps indicated, but may not require complete exit from the industry as such. I recall an interesting conversation that I heard, between the young scion of a minor industrial house and his elderly business acquaintance. The wise, elderly man was telling the daring young-ster, 'now that the government has allowed all these MNCs in, it is important for us to become their C&F agents or distributors. Recognise and embrace the loyal woman of steady and growing trading business; and do not run after the young thing in the red frock and start thinking you can compete or become a global player.' Thus the prodigal traders return to trade, from their prolonged sojourn as industrialists.

Pattern III

Quit When Quitting is Good, and Search Greener Pastures

Here, the management is proactive but has now realised that the environment has changed and that has made their extant business one of continuously falling profits. In all probability this manage-ment may rue that someone has moved their cheese and may also romance with things like Bombay Club or the SJM for a short while. But soon they will look for other cheese stations. In other words, they will exit the industry and enter other businesses. Does Chauhan's exit from the soft drinks' line, and subsequent empha-sis on Bisleri as well as the biscuit line, suggest such behaviour? Perhaps it does.

Pattern IV

Have Guts, Will Grow

Here, the proactive management of a firm notes that while the environment has become tougher, the long-term profitability of their extant business is not much in doubt. Hence they devote themselves to enhancing their competencies and focus on their business with redoubled vigour. These men and women look the global players in the eye and, at times, make the giants blink. They may of course adopt tactically easier paths (such as focusing on easier third world markets and perhaps entering the first world with low value items) to grow: but their long-term intent is to become global players themselves. The behaviour of Dr Reddy's Laboratories, Ranbaxy, and CIPLA in drugs' line or of TVS group in the auto components line, etc. reflects this pattern of behaviour.

REFERENCES

Alisson Graham T; *Essensce of Decision*, Harvard University Press, 1971.

Ansoff H Igor; *Corporate Strategy*, Mcgraw Hill, New York, 1965.

Baghai, M; Coley, S; and White, David; *The Alchemy of Growth*, OUP, New Delhi, 2000.

Cyert, R; and March, JG; *Behavioural Theory of the Firm*, Prentice-Hall, Englewood Cliffs, NJ, 1963.

Das, Gurucharan; *The Problem in Seminar*, p. 482, October 1999.

Datta, S; *Family Business in India*, Response Books, New Delhi, 1996.

Galbraith, JK; *Almost Everyone's Guide to Economics*, Penguin, London, 1978.

Gersoski, PA and Gregg P; *Coping With Recession*, Cambridge University Press, Cambridge, 1997.

Ghoshal, S; Piramal, Gita; and Bartlett, C; *Managing Radical Change*, Penguin, New Delhi, 2000.

Iyer, Lalita; *The Strategic Business Spiral*, Response Books, New Delhi, 2000.

Khandwala, PN; *Effective Corporate Response to Liberalization, the Indian Case, Social Engineer*, 1996:2.

Levitt, T; *Marketing Myopia*, HBR, 1956.

Merton, RK; *Social Theory and Social Structure*, Amerind, New Delhi, 1968.

Mittra, Kaveri; 'Remaking Duncans', *Business India*, 2 November 1998.

Ninan, TN; 'Chequered Past, Uncertain Future', in *Seminar*, October 1999.

Palande, PS; *Coping with Liberalisation: The Industry's Response to New Competition*, Response Books, New Delhi, 2000.

Phansalkar, SJ; *Making Growth Happen*, Response Books, New Delhi, 1999.

Phansalkar, SJ; *How Not to Ruin Your Small Industry*, Response Books, New Delhi, 1996.

Phansalkar, SJ; and Gulati, VP; *Oilseeds and Edible Oil Economy of India*, Vikas, New Delhi, 1994.

Piramal, Gita; *Business Maharajas*, Viking, New Delhi, 1996.

Phansalkar, SJ; and Mardikar, Sachin; 'Weathering the Storm', ICICI Research Centre, 2002.

Phansalkar, SJ; and Sriram, MS; 'Business development services for small enterprises—a study of Hyderabad, India, Small Enterprise Development', 12:1, June 2001.

Porter, M; *Competitive Strategy*, Free Press, New York, 1980.

Radhakrishnan, N; and Dutta, S; 'Despair and Hope', *Business India*, 9 March 1998.

Roy, S; 'Strategic Response of Firms to Economic Liberalization', FPM Thesis submitted to IIM Ahmedabad, 2002.

Ruttan, M; 'A historical and comparative view on the studies of Indian Entrepreneurship' *Economic Sociology*, 3:2, February 2002.

Samuelson, Paul A and Nordhaus, William; *Microeconomics*, McGraw-Hill, 2001.

Sekhar, RC; *Ethics in Business*, Response Books, New Delhi, 1997.

Steinbruner; *Cybernetic Theory of The Firm*, Princeton University Press, Princeton, NJ, 2002.

Tilak, Bal Gangadhar; *Geeta Rahasya*, p. 64 (original Marathi), KB Dhawale Prakashan, Mumbai, 1964.

Thompson, JD; *Organizations in Action*, Prentice-Hall, Englewood Cliffs, NJ, 1967.

Tripathi, Dwijendra; 'Change and Continuity', *Seminar*, October 1999.

Tripathi, Dwijendra; and Mehta, Makarand; *Business Houses in Western India*, Manohar, New Delhi, 1990.

Weiner, Norbert; *Collected Works*, MIT Press, 2001.

INDEX

ab initio, 87
ACC, 113
Access Deficit Charges, 58
accountability, 93
accumulation, 84
adaptive mechanism, 83
Administered Price Mechanism
    (APM), 24
adulteration, 68–69
advertisements, 126
Ambani's, 73, 77
Americans, 85
Amul, 80
anticipation, 84
Aquaguard, 124
Arthashastra, 66
Ashok Leyland, 113, 189
assessment of strategy, 84,
    117–21
asset specificity, 186, 189, 192
assured welfare schemes, 200
astigmatism, 186
attrition, 200
Avalon, 159
Ayodhya issue, 23

BPL, 45
BPOs, 46, 78
backward integration, 196; by
    buyers, 109–10
Bajaj, 45, 54, 64, 78, 193

Bangurs, 104
bania, 61, 62, 104
banking, 40
bankruptcy, 97
bargaining and monitoring, 88
barriers, 166
BASIX, 107
behavioural patterns, response,
    34, 51, 181
Bhagwat Gita, 66
Bharat Bijlee Motors, 25
Bharat Heavy Electricals Limited
    (BHEL), 53
Bharat Sanchar Nigam Limited
    (BSNL), 55
biaxially oriented poly-propylene
    (BOPP), 140, 154–55, 162, 165,
    167–68, 170, 175–77, 193;
    Indian scenario, 177–79;
    international scenario, 177
Bicon, 127, 128
Biocon, 54
Birlas, 54, 59, 74, 104, 129
Bisleri, 218
black marketing, 44
black money, 72, 77
Board for Industrial and
    Financial Reconstruction
    (BIFR), 72, 79, 192–93, 180
bohra, 61
Bombay Club, 26, 49, 218, 206

bootstrapping, 110, 134–36, 203, 209

bottlenecks, 87

bribes, 44

budget control, 96

bureaucracy, 79, 214

business development service (BDS), 189, 190–91

Business India, 56

business process re-engineering (BPR), 160

business strategy, 91

business valuation, 71

business-to-business (B2B), 70

business-to-consumer (B2C), 70

buyer, dependence on, 186, 192

C&F system, 205

CTV, 78

capacity expansion, build-up, 50, 63, 131, 161

capacity utilisation, 117, 156, 165

capital formation, 84

capital market reforms, 25

capitalism, 58, 60–61

castes, 58

Chaturvarna vyavastha, 58

Chaturvedi, 192

chettiar, 61, 62

Cipla, 219

circularity, 137–38

Cismo Plantgene, 154

classical contingency theory, 32

Close Up, 106

cohesion, 160

cold rolled grain oriented (CRGO), 92

colonial rule, 59

Combiflam, 197

commitment, 93, 95, 161, 203, 216

commodity management, 203

Common Minimum Programme (CMP), 19

communication, 57, 161

community welfare, 92

Companies Act, 53

Company Depot system, 205

compatibility, 123

competence, 138, 193, 204

competition, competitiveness, 21, 24, 28, 32, 37–38, 40–41, 50, 61, 71, 98, 105, 108, 109, 112–15, 130–31, 154, 165, 166, 178, 181–82, 197, 212, 215–16; domestic, 26, 73; international, 26, 73, 78; natural and strategic, 82–86

competitive advantage, 110, 205

competitive edge, 98, 107–08; based on bootstrapping, 134–36

competitive strategy, 30, 33

complacence, 72–73, 115, 178, 181–82

components, balancing, 86–88

conceptual continuum, 183

confidence, 203

Congress, 22

congruence, 34

consistency, internal, 95–97, 124–25

consolidation, 37

consumer behaviour, 106, 115

consumer loyalty, 50

contamination, 114

contingencies, 89–90

contingency plan, 32, 36, 125

contract enforcement, 88

control, 125–26

control loop adjustment, 35–37

cooperative strategies, 33

coordination costs, 86, 88–90, 212

coping mechanisms, 127, 210

COPU, 54–55

Core Parentals Ltd., 131

core strategy, 93, 104

corporate governance, 71

corporate strategy, 120

corrective action, 180
corruption, 44, 72
Cosmic, 161
Cosmo Ferrites, 154
Cosmo Films Limited (CFL),
    153; background, 154;
    beginning, 154–55; domestic
    markets, 164–65; exports,
    165–66; finance, 157–59;
    marketing and R&D, 163–64;
    organisation, 159–62, strategic
    planning groups (SPG), 154,
    156, production, 162–63;
    time-line of events, 167–70
Cosmo International (US) Inc.,
    170
Cosmo International Limited,
    Mauritius, 170
Cosmo Today, 161
cost cutting, reduction, 36, 74, 80
cost effectiveness, 63
cost leadership, 116
credit period, 117
credit recovery, 156
Crompton, 64
culture and tradition, 49, 59, 62, 92
Cumin's India Limited, 102
current account convertibility, 23
customer persuasion, 92, 166
customer support through
    service centers, 121
customisation, 166
cybernetic theory, 35, 37
cynicism, 92, 130

DCL polyesters, 74
Dabur, 45, 78
Daewoo, 121
dairy industry, delicensing, 23
debtor turnover, 132
decentralisation, 214
decision-making, 34–35, 55–56,
    79, 95, 100, 117, 127, 136, 159,
    180, 185, 210, 214

Deere, John, 133
delegation, 191
demand and supply, 36; gap, 40
democratic structures, 115
demographic factors, 86
dependability, 70
depreciation, 120
depression, 38
despair, 19
Dhanvantari Malam, 181, 193;
    evolution, 194–95; finance,
    198–99; human resource
    management, 200;
    manufacturing and logistics,
    195–96; marketing, 197–98;
    new business, 200–01;
    research and development,
    199–200
Dhara, 68
dharma, 57
differentiation, 85, 115–16
Dinshaw, 107
diplomacy, 139
discretion, 90–92, 210
dishonesty, 66
distribution chain, 197
distrust, 66, 191, 209
diversification, 41, 42, 105, 208;
    unrelated, 74, 76–80, 181
divestment process, 20
domain consensus, 102–03
domestic market, 61, 154, 164–65
dominant coalition, 86
downsizing, 74
Dr Reddy's Laboratories (DRL),
    54, 74, 79–80, 104, 127, 128,
    219
dummy firms, proliferation,
    76–77, 186, 193
dumping, 157
Dutt Committee of Enquiry, 113
Dwiwedi, Nagendranath, 194,
    198, 200–01
dynamism, 20, 21

ERP implementation, 163, 169–70
East India Company, 27
East-Asian crisis, 1997,
    meltdown, 23, 27
e-chaupals, 80
economic changes and recession,
    46–47, 130, 202, 205; industry
    response, 36–42
economic conditions, realities,
    21, 39, 48, 115, 121
economic morass, 20
economic opportunities, 47
economic policy, 49–50, 215, 217
economic power, concentration,
    60
economic reforms, 22
economy, 20, 23, 27, 50, 56, 60,
    121, 129, 186; dominance of
    government, 26
edible oil prices, 22
effectiveness, 161, 181
efficiency, operational efficiency,
    36, 38, 130–32, 135, 170, 203,
    211
Eicher, 107, 210
electronic media, 182
employment, 85, 183
entrepreneurship,
    entrepreneurial traits, 58–59,
    182, 184
entry barriers, 112
entry deterring price, 114
environmental factors, 50, 96–97,
    115, 122, 123–24
equality, 98
equity, 71, 93, 141, 157
Escorts, 45
Essar, 45
ethics, 193, 214
ethos, 68–71, 79
Eureka Forbes, 116
ex-ante assessment, 121
Excel, 106
exclusivity, 116

exit barriers, 112–13
exit strategy, 125
expansion, 41, 192
export-import policies, 40
exports, 165–66
external factors, 96–97

facelessness, 135
faith, 161
family managed companies,
    family business, 53–57, 59–66,
    73–79, 139, 194, 202, 206–10,
    214–15
fast moving consumer goods
    (FMCG), 56, 125, 164, 197
Federation of Indian Chambers
    of Commerce and
    Industry (FICCI), 65
feudalism, 72, 210
fidelity, 34
finance decisions, 39, 60, 141,
    157–59, 185, 191
First World, 114
fixed asset, 190
Flax Industries, 128, 192
flexibility, 95, 161, 163, 167, 192,
focus, 116–17
Ford, 121
Ford, Henry, 100
forecasting, 84
foreign direct investment (FDI),
    24
Foreign Exchange Regulation
    Act (FERA) regime, 54
foreign investment, 40
forward integration by
    suppliers, 110–11
fraternity, 98
free market, 98

GKW, 110–11
GSM telephony, 74
Gates, Bill, 111
generalisation, 184

generally accepted accounting
principles (GAAP), 67
generic competitive strategies, 39
geographic expansion, 107
Global Positioning Record
System (GPRS), 124
global vs local, 46, 56
goals, 31–33, 35, 37, 92–93, 107,
120–21
Goenka, 54, 104
Golden Quadrangle, 25
good corporate governance, 161
governance, 210, 215
Great Patron, 207
Greenfield projects, 23
growth, 41, 85, 88, 90–92, 98,
104–07, 121, 192, 210
Gujarat Ambuja Cement, 54
Gulf War, 22, 131

Hay's systems, 160
heterogeneity, 32
hierarchy, 51, 62, 140, 207
Hindustan Lever Limited (HLL),
106–07, 108, 165
homogeneity, 32–33
Honda, 108, 121
honesty, 101, 160
HopNskip, 193, 196, 197, 198,
201
human resources, 161–62
humility, 120
Hyundai, 121

ICICI Bank Limited, 21
Ideax, 196, 197, 198
implementation, 97
incentives, 200
inconsistency, 95–96, 124
incorporation, 88–90
incrementalism, 79, 81
India Motors, 121
Indian business and ethics of
business, 66

Indian Farmers and Fertilizers
Cooperative Ltd. (IFFCO), 78
Indian Tobacco Company (ITC),
80, 113
Indica, 80
indigenisation, 94
industrial depressions, 21
industrial licensing regime,
24, 40
informal business, 190
information and knowledge, 210
Information Technology (IT), 47
Infosys, 54
infrastructure bottlenecks, 79
innovation, 192; in operating
technological systems, 132–34
integration, 63, 89; See also
backward integration,
forward integration
intellectual property rights (IPR),
24, 108
intensity, 113
inter personal relationship,
159–60
interaction, 160
internal control orientation, 71–72
international market, 166
International Monetary Fund
(IMF), 22, 39
involvement, 113

Jaipuria, Ashok, 154–57
Jaipuria, Sitaram, 154
Jhunjhunwala, 54
job description, 160
joint stock companies, 56
joint ventures, 218
just in time, 131
Jyoti, 110–11

Kalnirnaya, 128
Kapoor, Sanjeev, 110
Kargil War, 19, 24
Kautilya, 66

kayasth, 61
Khetan, 55, 64
kinship, 62, 193, 200, 207–08
Kirloskars, 54, 55, 58
Kirloskar Cummins, *See* Cumin's India Limited

labour legislation, 23, 217
Lal, Vikram, 210
large business houses (LBH), 54, 56, 104
lateral entry, 111–12
law enforcement, 70, 72
leadership, 21, 24
Left, 19
legacy, 76
liberalisation, 26–27, 39, 40–42, 45, 49, 54, 74, 130, 202, 206
licensing regime, 61, 113
Life Insurance Corporation (LIC), 53
liquidation losses, 113
liquidity, 23, 95, 117
Liril soap, 106
lobbying, 114
local vs global, *See* global vs local
logistics, 121, 131, 139, 140, 195–96

M-seal, 107
Mafatlal, 54
Maharashtra Housing and Area Development Authority (MHADA), 94–95
Mahendra, 54
maladjustment, 180
management agency system, 63
management, management theory, 49, 65–66, 69–73, 78, 90, 97, 105, 125–26, 129, 136, 160, 186, 203, 212, 216–18
Marigold, 197, 198

marketability, 41
market, marketing, 37, 95–96, 121–23, 166, 181–82, 191, 193; vs manufacturing, 159; myopia, 186; and R&D, 163–64; size, 78
Maruti Udyog Limited (MUL), 121, 122
marwari, 61, 104, 120
Mastek, 127
McClelland, 58–59
McKinsey, 80
means, 93–95
media-mix, 94
MELTRON, 53
mercantile capitalism, 103, 107, 208, 209, 214
mergers and acquisitions, 38
MidDay, 116
middle class, 96
mindset change, 215
mindset issues, 161, 178, 185–94
Mission and Market vs Money Management, 64
Mittal, Atul, 161
Mittal, Sushil Kumar, 154, 156–67, 169, 178
mixed economic model, 39
Modis, 104
money-lender, 62, 103, 112
monitoring, 97
Monopolistic and Restrictive Trade Practices (MRTP) Act, 40, 54, 60, 63, 76, 104
monopoly, 33, 63
moral values, 71, 182
morale, 157
motivation, 59, 120, 209
Mukherjee, Ranbir, 156–63, 166–67
multinational corporations (MNCs), 20, 47, 53, 54, 56, 60, 78, 99, 218
Murugappa, 54

NPA Bill, 20, 199
n-ach theory, 58–59
Nanda, 54
National Dairy Development
    Board (NDDB), 53, 68, 90
National Institute of Information
    Technology (NIIT), 101–02
National Thermal Power
    Corporation (NTPC), 53
natural adaptation process, 83
natural growth, 85–86
nature, 85
Nav Bharat, 74
negative margins, 180
negotiation process, 33
new economic policy, 40
niche marketing, 116
non-business family entrepreneur
    run business, 54, 206
non-pecuniary values, 89
non-profit organisation, 109
non-quantitative restrictions
    (QR), 114
non-tariff, 24, 114

OTC, 195, 196, 197
obstinacy, 181
occupational choices, 59
oil-seed industry, 68–71
open appraisal system, 160
openness, 161, 209
operating technology and
    systems, 132–34
operational efficiency, See
    efficiency
opportunism, opportunistic
    behaviour, 28–29, 42–46, 56,
    81, 127, 140–41, 202, 205,
    214–15; cause of stagnation
    and failure, 207–13
optimism, 19–20, 23, 42
Orchid, 127
organisational culture,
    procedures, 39, 139, 141, 191

organisation theory framework, 31
organisational pettiness, 193
outsourcing, 25, 90, 95, 132, 205
over-capacity, 164
over-specification, 92

Param Atta, 107
parsi, 61
participation, participative
    methodology, 125, 160
patents, 166
paternalism, 140, 207
Paul, Lord Swaraj, 25
penetration, 106
Pepsi, 106
performance, 21, 28–29, 36,
    71–73, 126, 127, 128, 130–31,
    137–38, 140–41, 142, 192–94,
    203, 209, 213
pessimistic prognostication,
    pessimism, 19, 58
Pidilite, 107
planned economy, 63
planning action, 84
Planning Commission, 55
Pokhran blasts, 19, 23, 27
policy changes, shift, 21, 79
political dimension, 35
political fluidity, 22
political instability, uncertainty,
    20, 57
political realism, 23
politicians, 44, 126
poor coping, 181–82
populism, 20
positive discrimination, 20
power distribution, 25
Praj Industries, 128
price competitiveness, 71, 115
price-cutting, 117
price-quality product profile, 115
pricing, prices, 36, 37, 50, 97,
    121, 123, 164, 196
private sector, 20, 25, 60

pro-active behaviour, 136–40, 145, 209, 215–16, 218
probity, 67, 70
process regime, 80
product choice, 127–29, 131
product economics, 97
product features, 121
product improvement, 36
product life-cycle (PCL), 128–29, 203
productivity improvement, 130
product-market arena, 137, 140
product-market posture, 49, 98, 101–04, 107, 210
product mix, 70
product positioning, 116, 121, 147
product range widening , 42
product vs commodity, 64
production policy, 163
professional integrity, 98
professional management vs control orientation, 65
professionalism, 61, 65
profitability, profits, 71, 85, 158, 216, 218
promotion, promoters, 72–73, 121
propaganda cum distribution (PCD), 132
propensity, 86
proprietary firms to company, transition, 185
Protestant work ethic, 58
public interest notices, 100
public sector, public sector units (PSUs), 40, 53, 55, 56
Purohit, Banwarilal, 104
push-pull moves, 94

quality, 36, 41, 70, 95, 115, 121, 124, 126, 217
Quantitative Restrictions (QR), 49

ROCE, 145
Rakhunde, 160

Ranbaxy, 219
rationality, 32, 34, 87
Raymond, 64
recession, 36–42
red herring, 84
refocusing, 80
reforms, industry's response, 25–28
regulated foreign exchange regime, 23
regulation, 39, 113, 126, 185, 189, 203, 204
relative prices, 121
relative rewards, 107
reliability, 70
Reliance, Reliance Infocom, 77, 79
repositioning products, 80
resistance, 65
resource allocation, 31
resources, demand and supply, 33
respectability, 70
responsiveness, 160, 162
retrenchments, 99
retrofitting, 99
return on investment, 93
revealed preference approach, 120
reverse engineering, 80, 215
rightsizing, 74, 80, 90
risks, 116, 123, 140, 161; and resources, 125
Ruiyas, 74

sanctions, 23–24, 27
Sarabhai, 54
Satyam, 54, 133–34
schizophrenia, 212
secularism, 98
self-fulfillment, 105
sensitivity analysis, 125
shock therapy, 39
SIA-Tata combine, 114
sickness, 127, 183–85, 194
Siemens, 25
Simon, 34

Singh, Manmohan, 22
Singhania, 54
sinophobia, 27
situation-specific analysis and judgement, 122
slack, 87–88
small business enterprises, 53
Small Industry Development Corporation Limited (SIDCO), 94
Small Scale Enterprise (SSE), 184, 186, 189, 191
social hierarchy, order, 72, 200
social turmoil and uncertainty, 23
socio-political and institutional environment, 59
software development, 133, 182
solidarity, 70
species, 85
speculation, 190, 193, 208
spiritual dispensation, 59
Sriram, MS, 189
stabilisation process, 40
stagnation, 29, 105, 113, 127, 180–83, 204, 207–13
standard operating procedures, 34
State Bank of India (SBI), 65
stockpiling, 83
strategic behaviour, thinking, 21, 28, 56, 78, 82, 87, 108, 127, 115, 187, 191, 205, 207; vs opportunistic behaviour, 42–46
strategic-opportunistic dimension, 51
Structural Adjustment Process, 40
style, 100
subjugation, 214
subsidies, 24, 40, 206
subsistence mode, 84
substitute products, 111
Sudha Oil Industries, 134–36
sugar industry, 27

Sumangal Prakashan, 128
Sumo, 105
Sun, 134
Sun Pharmaceuticals, 54, 106, 127
Sundrop, 69
supply chain, 94, 123
support capacity, 33
Surf, 106
surplus, 136
sustainable growth, 39
swadeshi, 41, 49
Swadeshi Polytex, 154
SWOT (Strength, Weakness, Opportunities, Threats) analysis, 121–23
sycophancy, 193
symbiotic relationship, 40
synergy, 98, 108–09
systematisation, 141, 210

TVS group, 219
tariffs, 50, 215
Tata Chemicals, 90
Tata Consultancy Services (TCS), 134
Tata Iron and Steel Company Limited (TISCO), 111
Tata Motors, 105–07, 120–21
Tatas, 47, 54, 59, 64, 79, 104
tax evasion, 68, 72
tax liability, 193, 204
taxation, tax regime, 40, 67–68, 72, 123, 203, 214
team work, 140–41, 191, 210
technology, 89, 90, 107, 112, 129
Telco, *See* Tata Motors
thought process, 184
Thums Up, 55
total quality management (TQM), 159
trade barriers, 114
trade credits, 94
training, 120
transparency, 160, 162

transaction costs, 88
transaction related services, 186, 190–91
transformation, 28, 80
transition process, 185
transparency, 67, 72, 80, 141, 167, 209–10, 212
treasury opportunism, 45
trust, 57, 70, 207

uncertainties, 89
underperformance, 71–72, 80
Union Carbide, 55
unique selling proposition (USP), 131
unrelated diversification, 107

vaisya, 58, 66
value migration, 78, 81
values in management, value orientation, 66, 98–101, 123, 125

vani, 61
vested interests, 43, 48, 206
viability, 97
Vicks, 197, 198
Vim, 106

wage employment, 184
West: cultural aggression, 67
Wheel, 106, 111
WIPRO, 46, 77, 90
wireless in local loop (WiLL), 111
wisdom, 50
work ethics, 58
working capital, 130, 186, 190, 203
World Bank, 19, 39, 40
World Trade Organisation (WTO), 24, 27

Y2K, 46, 78